SHADOW THE PITCH

THE LONG SUMMER OF 2017-18

GIDEON HAIGH

Published by:
Wilkinson Publishing Pty Ltd
ACN 006 042 173
Level 4, 2 Collins Street
Melbourne, Vic 3000
Ph: 03 9654 5446
www.wilkinsonpublishing.com.au

NATIONAL
LIBRARY
OF AUSTRALIA

A catalogue record for this
book is available from the
National Library of Australia

Planned date of publication: 08-2018
Title: Shadows on the Pitch
ISBN(s): 9781925642520 : Printed - Paperback

Design by Spike Creative Pty Ltd
Ph: (03) 9427 9500
spikecreative.com.au

CONTENTS

INTRODUCTION

Cricket summers are getting longer, to the extent that the notion is almost redundant. The expression 'summer game' barely captures it any longer — in Australia the sport has spread through spring, abides through autumn, continues to pivot on Christmas and New Year, but somehow goes on straining for engagement and event. Dirk Diggler never had to climax so regularly and on cue.

That can lead to a degree of monotony, of scenarios and personnel — although not in the protracted season of 2017-18. The Australian men's cricket team arrived in Bangladesh in mid-August 2017 and departed South Africa in mid-April 2018, having deployed thirty-seven players in eleven Tests, ten one-day internationals and seven T20 internationals. They came from behind to draw a series in Asia; they regained the Ashes, rising from fifth to third in the world's Test championship; they slipped to fourth on the ODI table and rose to second in the T20I rankings. But the souring of the achievements began around 3pm on 24 March 2018 at Newlands, when umpires summoned Cameron Bancroft to discuss attempts to alter the condition of the 42-over-old ball to which they had been alerted.

Ten weeks earlier, Bancroft had posed on a stage at the Sydney Cricket Ground celebrating victory over England; within two weeks, he and three of his fellow revellers, captain Steve Smith, vice-captain David Warner and coach Darren Lehmann, had become casualties of perhaps the angriest and suddenest sports controversy of the century. They were execrated by prime ministers, pilloried by the public, lashed and lampooned on social media, hounded and heckled even in airports — paid back, some would say, in their own coin, for Australians down the decades have been quick to insist that theirs is the right way to play. In certain circles, there was an acute sense of betrayal. The newspaper that had anointed Smith its Australian of the Year less than two months before now demanded his sacking — and I should know because it was the newspaper, *The Australian*, for which I work.

This collection distils from my daily reporting the essence of that protracted 2017-18, concentrating on Australia's home series with England, which I saw firsthand, and away series in South Africa, which I observed from a distance. Both featured excellent cricket, the former also stages of humdrum, the latter also gashes of ugliness. The balance of calm and the memorable in cricket is ever elusive. Cricket is a game replete with restraints, but at its most exciting trends towards chaos. In March and April, it arrived there and stayed a while. The consequences are yet to play out but will shape the season of 2018-19 — which will be on us before we know it.

Gideon Haigh
May 2018

ENGLAND, THEY'RE ENGLAND

24 October 2017

Even George Orwell found it confusing. 'We call our islands by no fewer than six different names,' he complained. 'England, Britain, Great Britain, the British Isles, the United Kingdom and, in very exalted moments, Albion'. In his canonical wartime essay 'England, Your England', Orwell decided that it was this first variation he preferred. So has cricket.

Not exclusively, of course. For three-quarters of the 20th century, English cricket teams toured under the rubric of the Marylebone Cricket Club — male only throughout that time and run by committees that proverbially made Tory cabinets look like Trotskyists.

The teams have been led by Scots, Irishmen and Welshmen, by men born in Sydney, Bengaluru, Milan, Lima, Queenstown and Johannesburg. Now they are coached by an Australian. But the squad led by Joe Root arriving in Perth tomorrow will be known only as 'England' and identified by the St George's Cross which its Barmy Army auxiliary will loyally flourish, with the reinforcement of an additional syllable ('Eng-er-land').

Somehow, praise be, this still works. From afar, 'England' can appear a small, seething and isolated island, permanently estranged from the continent, worseningly befuddled by the United States, tenuously connected to its former Commonwealth, and wracked internally by the forces of devolution: a kind of hollowed-out brand name trading on old loyalties and obsolete impressions.

Hereabouts it is commonly identified with the quaint, the antique, the archaic. The London-born, Oxford-educated Australian prime minister who marked his reinstatement of knights and dames by honouring a nonagenarian duke achieved the equivalent of six sixes in an over of anachronism.

In cricket terms, nonetheless, 'England' remains curiously immutable: the team of Grace and Hobbs, of Jardine and Larwood, of Snow and Boycott, of Botham and Gower, and perhaps today of Anderson and Broad. This summer portends a mid-table clash, between third and fifth on the International Cricket Council Test Rankings. But all that will matter is the Ashes ladder of two.

In this sense, however, Test cricket's original rivalry is having to do a lot of heavy lifting. For a time, it was fashionably contrary to invoke India v Pakistan as cricket's definitive head-to-head contest. Politics has steadily ruled that out, and cricket's two most populace nations have not met across five days for a decade. The last time the Ashes were contested here, by contrast, they had been brought forward to form part of a cycle of ten consecutive Tests, three of which were as dead as the Norwegian Blue. The players were left half-dead too.

This summer represents a different kind of doubling down on the mystique of 'England': it's the first time in this country that the women's Ashes have been offered as a prelude to the men's. Ironically, for the first sixty-four years of women's international cricket, Australian and English teams studiously abjured the Ashes, seeking to emphasise the game ahead of the rivalry. Then, as Raf Nicholson explored in an excellent piece for *Cricinfo* a couple of weeks ago, a miniature bat was burned in a low-key ceremony at Lord's. Presto: instant heritage.

There's a bit of this about too. During the Perth Test, Channel 9 will broadcast a three-part Cricket Australia series about the Ashes — what might be called a docutisement, entitled 'Forged in Fire'. If we're to be pedantic about it, the essence of the Ashes is that they are funerary remains, and therefore cold. The original *Sporting Times* death notice was as much of a joke about cremation — still taboo but gaining advocates and verging on legality — as it was about cricket. But cricket marketing loves combustion: think #TheFurnace, Perth Scorchers, Brisbane Heat, Queensland Fire etc. And maybe that is the point — that 'England', 'The Ashes', even 'Australia' must now coexist with the values of the mass market let rip in the Big Bash League, and big and bashing sport generally.

Already what protects the Ashes has at least as much to do with cents as sentiment: cricket series involving Australia and England are guaranteed money-spinners. They connect satisfyingly with the public, offering the consolations of continuity, the satisfactions of ritual, the transgressive pleasures of no-holds-barred competition within boundaries of formality. They are the standard against which all Australia's bilateral cricket relationships are judged.

In general, however, bilateral cricket is weak — thus the championships foreshadowed two weeks ago by the ICC. And in the inaugural cycle of the championship's Test component scheduled to begin with the next Ashes, the value of matches between England and Australia looks like being effectively diluted. Under the mooted scoring system, Test rubbers will be worth 100 points: 60 for the winner, 40 to be divided among individual Test outcomes. The minimum length of a 'series' will be two Tests, from which can be inferred that this will become the default. That being so, say a Bangladesh v New Zealand Test in Dunedin, being one of two, will be worth more points than an Ashes Test at Lord's, being one of five.

The other emergent competition is domestic. An advantage the Ashes has always enjoyed is the kind of self-reinforcing deference towards it — the sense that Australia v England brings the rest of the cricket world to an attentive standstill, making for the laying down of deep memories. The world stops now for nobody and nothing. This summer more than 100 games of men and women's BBL commence just after the Second Test, and continue four weeks after the Fifth Test. It's far from clear who will be the accompaniment for whom.

Longer-term, a reckoning is overdue with the reality of 'England', in the context of Brexit, and also Australia, perhaps in the guise of a republic, but certainly in an age of greater cultural diversity and more portable allegiance. David Warner looks like the archetypal Aussie, but opening partner Matt Renshaw, born in England, could easily have numbered among his opponents.

Change and its attendant insecurities may cause us to cling more tightly to our ancient totems — and illusions, as Orwell observed, can be so powerful as to bend conduct toward them. But symbols need to renew as well as to re-old, as it were, and the Ashes' proven resilience is no guarantee of their future relevance.

AUSTRALIAN SELECTION

THE CHOSEN AND THE CHOOSERS

17 November 2017

Whomever had this particular Australian Test team in your office sweep deserves their win. But they should have to pay for beers.

Having spread like one of those budgets leaked so extensively by Laurie Oakes as to leave nothing to actually report on the day itself, the combination provoked as many questions as answers, not so much about its composition as the philosophy underlying it.

What were those oh-so-important first three rounds of Sheffield Shield cricket about then? Shaun Marsh averaged 39 across those games — he'd probably go on averaging 39 after an alien invasion. Yet here he is, an evergreen thirty-four-years-young, ahead of 29-year-old Glenn Maxwell, a superior fielder who bowls and has a better fitness record while still to play a Test in his own country.

Where Shield form mattered, by contrast, was in the choice of David Warner's partner, Matthew Renshaw, having stretched 70 runs across 288 balls in half a dozen hits, giving way to Cameron Bancroft, after consecutive innings of 76, 86 and an unbeaten 228. Yet Bancroft himself had had a patchy time up to that sudden surge. Apart from a double-hundred for Gloucestershire two months ago, he had averaged 28 in first-class cricket across the year. Through that time, Renshaw was battling bravely through six Tests in the sub-continent.

And Tim Paine? One wishes him well: he has been an unlucky cricketer who has always looked the part. But his nickname, 'Kid', is now as incongruous as Michael Clarke's, 'Pup'. Paine is about to turn thirty-three. He did not start the season in his own state side; he is not his state's first-choice keeper. He averages less than 30 in first-class cricket; in the last four seasons less than 20; he has made one century in 91 matches, where Peter Nevill last season made two in two.

In what sense has he banged the door down, as distinct from leaving his runners by the mat? And what would national selector Trevor Hohns's predecessor Rod Marsh think of picking someone to keep wickets for five sticky Brisbane days a week after his standing at slip in a Shield match under mackerel skies in Melbourne?

Alas, poor Nevill, brought in to a losing Australian team as a locum thirty months ago, forced to find his way with a battling attack, and his batting slot between struggling Mitches, Marsh and Starc. But sometimes your face doesn't fit, or maybe in Nevill's case his mouth, judged insufficiently ornery by his captain.

So we're presented with performance picks that aren't really underpinned by performance, horses chosen for ill-defined courses.

Perhaps this is a function of the greater volatility of modern performance — which tends to vertiginous peaks, poorer consistency, and in this way causes consistency to trade at a discount.

Perhaps it reflects a desire to convey that places are available and competition open — which could just as easily instil senses of entitlement as of opportunity.

Now, there is a place for brainstorms. Selection is as much a human process as playing and coaching, factoring intuition, memory, skills of comparison, knowledge of technique. Selectors develop preferences and aversions — athletic, aesthetic, ideological, moral. The currency of runs and wickets is meant to be non-negotiable, but often as not is sought as verification of a pre-existing hunch.

Just at the moment, however, Hohns' panel of coach Darren Lehmann, national talent manager Greg Chappell and television commentator Mark Waugh seems in almost as much a state of flux as its team. A lack of clarity surrounds its objectives, principles and even its future.

Interestingly, *Cricinfo* this week ran with a well-sourced story heralding changes to Cricket Australia's approach to selection, high-performance chief Pat Howard favouring the application of a model more centralised and streamlined, based on collaborations of coaches and talent managers — something like this already prevails in New South Wales. It is alleged to create an environment more rigorous, more 'accountable'.

But does it? Looked at another way, the coaches and talent managers are essentially being positioned to grade their own work, with the risk of rewarding those who pay obeisance to the system rather than those who exercise independent judgement.

There's a reason selection panels in Australia traditionally operated at a remove from the day-to-day. It helped objectivity; it tempered parochialism and personal sentiment.

That dynamic changed with the push to professionalise what had been honorary functions by including ex officio members — coaches, captains, managers etc. 'Accountability' is every suit's wet dream; in theory none could be against it; in practice it is mainly about having someone in the structure to shift blame onto.

Cricinfo also reported Howard as favouring 'the use of deep statistical analysis and computer-based modelling to judge the suitability of players.' It's a kite he's flown for some years, and has a good deal to commend it in shorter forms of the game, where domestic T20 franchises are always fossicking for salient indicators of success. Yet data is a good servant and a bad master — especially, one suspects, in formats as complex and layered as first-class and Test cricket, and with men and women coming to personal as well as professional maturity at differing rates.

Howard is an energetic and dedicated executive with an admirable willingness to challenge established ideas. But if we're to start talking about 'accountability', Australia's away record during his tenure (13 Test wins and 20 defeats, 31 one-day wins and 37 defeats) hardly made an unassailable case for the recent extension of his contract. And every so often he sounds like Robert McNamara, LBJ's defence secretary, who kept advising that the US was winning the Vietnam War by every numerical measure.

In the short-term of these Ashes, it should not matter. England are modest opponents. Mitchell Starc, Josh Hazelwood and Patrick Cummins will be no less menacing for a few marginal picks, especially starting [summer] at a venue where Australia have won 21 and lost none of their last 28 Tests. It's an irony of this summer that Australian cricketers if they regain the Ashes will shore up an administration from whom they were recently estranged. Well, it always *was* a partnership ….

Further down the track, circumstances grow a good deal less clear. Australia conclude this protracted summer with four away Tests against South Africa, who will meantime have been toughened by hosting India. By the last of those matches, at the Wanderers, Steve Smith's team could look very different again.

TO ABSENT FRIENDS

21 November 2017

The battle of Waterloo was proverbially won on the playing fields of Eton. Will the Ashes of 2017-18 be recalled as surrendered in the dimly-lit streets of Bristol, in the vicinity of the mBargo nightclub?

Seven years ago, Andrew Strauss led England to a rare retention of the Ashes Down Under, and knows better than most how much must go right to curb Australian rampancy in their own conditions. As England's director of cricket, he has proven a cautious incrementalist, prepared to trust his players as 'adults', including a promotion for the mercurial Stokes to within a Joe Root back spasm of the national captaincy.

Yet even in this micro-managing, macro-monied age, the best-laid plans can be set at nought by a minute's red mist. In his minute, Stokes threw fifteen punches, which might as well have been into his own head once they were caught on CCTV. Stokes, a talisman in the Ashes of 2015 and in his sporting prime at twenty-six, was the sole member of England's team for which Australia had no effective counter, potentially as influential as Mitchell Johnson four years ago. Now Australia did not need to come up with one. England's steep challenge became nearly vertical.

We identify Ashes with great on-field achievements; it's easy to overlook how they have been shaped by absences. Sometimes this manifests simply in the veneer of a series. Cricket Australia's promotional campaign for the last Ashes Down Under featured an outback photo shoot with David Warner, Mitchell Starc and James Pattinson. In the event only Warner played; Starc and Pattinson were both hors de combat, the last having played just four Tests since.

But precisely because they are great, the best players shift power balances. The Ashes of 1974-75 will forever be associated with the fearsome combination of Dennis Lillee and Jeff Thomson. Yet would they have had it all their own way had England's selectors not omitted John Snow and alienated Geoff Boycott, their matchwinners four years earlier? 1981 remains the summer of 'Botham's Ashes'. But would he have dominated an Australia reinforced by Greg Chappell, who world wearily opted out of the tour, appetite for cricket dulled by the sourness surrounding the underarm ball?

This is the downside of outstanding cricketers. They create dependences; they nurture cults. Even Botham grew burdensome as his career tapered in its last five years. After England retained the Ashes in the Boxing Day Test of 1986, he averaged 20.57 with the bat and 57.52 with the ball, a name ever noisier, a threat ever emptier. Australia, moreover, has been a graveyard of reputations, perhaps the worst locale to undertake that one tour too many, as Walter Hammond found in 1946-47, Trevor Bailey, Godfrey Evans, and Frank Tyson in 1958-59, and Graeme Swann, Matt Prior, Tim Bresnan, Monty Panesar and possibly even Kevin Pietersen four years ago.

Stokes' absence, however, is more than a mere cricket story, for it is set to shape off-field as well as on-field perceptions. The most successful English team of this generation, Strauss's in 2010-11, succeeded by embracing Australia as a destination to enjoy. Strauss is married to an Australian; coach Andy Flower had played first-class cricket here; half a dozen others had played grade cricket in various states. This time coach Trevor Bayliss is Australian. But, because Stokes' night out drew in several teammates, he has placed his team under surveillance of mainstream and social media, including Bayliss, publicly indulgent of his players' relaxing out of hours. Multiple storms in tabloid teacups seem almost foreordained.

The irony is that Australia are themselves feeling absence, by attrition. Only three players survive from that heady whitewash four years ago, half as many as endure in the visitors' ranks. The batting rotates on the axis of captain Steve Smith and David Warner. The quest for a regular wicketkeeper and a useful all-rounder has returned pretty much to where it began. Players have just come through a disaffecting industrial dispute with their administrators; the Ashes itself will be rivalled by the ever-Bigger Bash League. It says something of the touring party's thrown-together quality that an Australian team so inconsistent, and ranked fifth in the world, goes into the series as such solid favourites.

Yet that is the way of it, and it is not a blame lightly shifted. Truth be told, England having enjoyed a single series victory Down Under in thirty years, Australia had history on their side long before Stokes went on his rampage. Now he is potentially that most valuable of figures in a debacle, a scapegoat, having undermined the careers of many of those he has played with and some whom he yet might. This is more than a standard sporting self-immolation; for Ben Stokes it may well be a personal Waterloo.

PREVIEW

WISHFUL THINKING

22 November 2017

The numbers have been crunched, the predictions are in, the trash has been talked, even by Nathan Lyon — 'Could we end some careers? I hope so.' England's 'scars' have been more closely analysed than on *Nip/Tuck*. There's broad consensus of what is to be expected in the Ashes of 2017-18. But what is to be hoped?

Cricket is often regarded as a romantic game. Yet it is reported, in the main, pragmatically, as a series of day-to-day issues, akin to political talking points. The accent is seldom on what one who loves cricket would actually like to see. Your indulgence please.

It has been a curious week in Australia. A national team has been selected in a way that has non-plussed many — not so much its composition, full as it is of honest strivers, as the seeming elasticity of concepts such as 'in form', 'out of form', 'class' and 'experience'.

Funnily enough, a still more severe wave of negativity followed the selection of England's touring squad two months ago. 'It's horrendous!' shrieked Kevin Pietersen. 'They may as well not go!'

Yet nobody in England felt it necessary to counsel ex-players and pundits that they should rally round Joe Root's team; nobody called it 'disappointing' that some were failing in their duty of 'being positive' and 'getting behind the boys', as here. Perhaps that is cricket's *vice anglais* — the English game's knack for self-flagellation. But it also seems just a little more robust than the underlying Australian attitude that too much cheerleading is not enough.

Cricket Australia's summer hashtag #BeatEngland is similarly canted. It must have taken a whole room of marketing consultants. But what is it? A cricketing citizenship test? Another semblance of football's bleed-for-the-club mentality?

One of cricket's abiding appeals is its generosity. When we gather, it is to celebrate the game every bit as much as victory. Generations of Australian cricket fans were turned onto the game by watching the epic West Indian teams of the 1980s. What sense would the hashtag #BeatWestIndies have made in that context?

The Ashes is a fierce rivalry, but also companionable. Sure, there will be some for whom 5-0 will not be a conclusive enough margin, and good luck to them. The most ardent Australian supporter I've ever known was a politics professor in Manchester born in Zimbabwe with an unappeasable craving for England's annihilation, who never ceased to deplore Adam Gilchrist's optimistic declaration at Headingley in 2001, who would cheerfully have had the series of 2006-7 extended to ten Tests. But it would surely be more memorable for this series if, for example, the rivals were two-all going into Sydney, or at least played out games that truly ebbed and flowed, tided and flooded, showcased skill, revealed character.

Too long for a hashtag, I guess. But while the national team may represent us, it is not the sole centre of allegiance. Darren Lehmann is a legend of Yorkshire whose brother-in-law earned thirty English caps, then coached Joe Root and Jonny Bairstow; thanks to his English mother, Steve Smith could today conceivably have been on the other side.

Every Test series these days being something of a referendum on the future of the format, there may have been greater need for events stirring and for individuals transcending. CA's CEO James Sutherland spread alarm a few weeks ago with remarks that Test cricket was 'just not commercially viable.' At the same time, cricket is not a listed company, has no hectoring shareholders to appease, no hurdle rate of return to meet, and to a great degree shapes its own market forces. The game somehow seems to cry poorer as it grows richer.

Whatever the case, the Ashes today is Test cricket incarnate, the format's other rivalry, India v Pakistan, having reached such a pitch of off-field antagonism that it no longer seems possible. The next time Australia and England meet they will initiate the cycle of the envisioned World Test Championship. This summer, then, is their last opportunity to influence how the five-day game faces that future.

It would be well, too, to take stock of our blessedness in being here. This weekend marks three years since Phillip Hughes was struck down at the Sydney Cricket Ground, and cricket was shaken to its core. It seems an aeon ago, if one is to judge from the sudden strange leering about fast bowlers being 'nasty', opponents being 'scared' and talk of 'ending careers'. But next Thursday would also have been Hughes's twenty-ninth birthday, and he would almost certainly have been at the Gabba with us. Between times England has lost James Taylor, a fine player whose health cost him his Ashes opportunities, aged just twenty-six.

Again, nothing to interest the face paint patriots or marketing gurus, but no less real for that. For every dream realised, many more are thwarted; fortune distributes unevenly, and the difference between success and failure can be measured in microns. If he's not everyone's idea of a paragon, David Warner seemed to have it pretty right a few days ago: 'We're all sportsmen. We're trying to achieve the same thing and that's to win. So I wish everyone good luck.' Ditto.

BRISBANE TEST DAY I

SETTLING IN

23 November 2017

Unknown knowns? Say hello to known unknowns.

Few England teams have arrived at a First Test so unheralded, almost incognito, 'nobodies' and 'no-names' being among the more generous descriptions. As far as many Australians were concerned, the visiting top three was Alastair Cook, Subject to Selection and Batty McBatface.

With their teammates, James Vince and Mark Stoneman had played three warm-up matches on pitches where bowling at speed was as rewarding as pushing rope. It looked to some educated observers like a honeytrap, designed to spring at the Gabba, with the revelation of twenty-two yards of fiery hell.

But if such a memo existed, it never reached Kevin Mitchell, whose pitch, under a sun too gentle to bake it hard, mocked the Australian muzzle velocities of around 140kmh. And so the anonymous Vince and Stoneman bedded in on the crucial variable of the surface, with promising security.

Since Australia chose its squad for Brisbane, England's objective has been correspondingly plain — to bat deep and long enough for the hosts to feel the want of a fifth bowler. Easier said than done, of course, and on the basis of their batting in the last year like planning for a bouffant having just a combover to work with.

Wispy and round-shouldered, Vince is the easiest of all England's batsmen on the eye, and had previously the lightest impact on scoreboards — seven matches without a half-century. When he reached his first yesterday by caressing Hazlewood through point, he offered his partner a perfunctory head-down handshake and his coaches a modest nod — of gratitude, one imagines, for his second chance.

His reputation has been for attractive strokes and arrested developments. Against the Cricket Australia XI in Adelaide, he fell in the first over of leg spin and the penultimate over of the first session aiming for cow corner. His edge eluded Tim Paine here, between accumulations of half his runs through the covers, as the Australian pace bowlers pursued lengths a tad full.

Stoneman: there can hardly have been a better name for an opening bat, reminiscent of the favourite boulder that Tracey Emin married on the grounds that 'it's not going anywhere'. He has been left in possession as Cook's partner as much by the form of others, Haseeb Hameed and Keaton Jennings losing their respective technical ways, as his own.

His method, however, is more robust and reassuring, without extensive preliminaries or obtrusive mannerisms, recalling another Surrey left-hander, John Edrich, who made a hundred first-class hundreds with a backlift that never rose above the height of the stumps.

Early on, Stoneman leaned out to slash wide past gully, at a distance where Edrich would have abjured a stroke until he was 150 — his county reputation is actually for liking the kiss of bat on ball.

Otherwise he played the ball under the eyes, soaking up the bowling and the circumstances patiently, dropping his wrists beneath bouncers, standing sentry over the off-side channel. When Cummins angled the ball back to bowl him in the last over before tea, it was against the run of play — actually the Australian's maiden first-class wicket at the Gabba.

To that point it was almost as though the home side had given it all at their strenuous press conferences over the preceding days. For all the talk of 2013-14, it is in cricket term dog years ago: at the toss stood Michael Clarke and Kevin Pietersen, turned by the intervening four years into grizzled veterans. Australian dominance in Brisbane was reinforced by the presence of referee Richie Richardson, a young dasher the last time a visiting team won a Test here, although that was another Gabba, and a rather different square, ago.

The coin falling Joe Root's way warded off the various Gabba omens. The sight of the ball making parabolae into Paine's gloves and the fall of a soothing rain then prolonged the hospitality. Taking the pitch out of the equation offered a way forward: it was no coincidence that the day's fastest delivery, from Mitchell Starc, was a full toss. The pitch was likewise an irrelevance when Nathan Lyon swooped and nonchalantly detonated the non-striker's stumps ahead of Vince's sliding bat.

Vince's intentions were pure — rotation, prudence, initiative, impetus. His technique was not bad, stunning the ball into the off-side and setting off with the momentum of his forward press. But Lyon was not at cover to rest. He is deceptively quick and agile, and these days confident in all his capabilities. Vince was shortly wishing to turn back time.

With this, the Englishmen went into their shells — withdrew into them like they were nautiluses, in fact, as the late-afternoon shadow of the stands engulfed the field. Root was subdued, Dawid Malan almost somnolent. With a loop and a smile, Lyon found bounce and deviation.

Despite best efforts, none of the top order had taken up coach Trevor Bayliss's injunction to turn 60s into 160s. It was a scenario for which the tourists would probably have settled amid the morning's unknowns, but not quite as encouraging on the basis of what had become known.

CAPTAIN ON PARADE
24 November 2017

On the first morning on the First Test, Steve Smith emerged for the toss approximately five minutes early. Though the field of play was typically thronged with promenading members of the lanyarded classes, he was momentarily unaccompanied, standing out in his whites, cap and blazer like the captain of a school's first XI. Wandering out, team sheet in his hand, he was alone in his thoughts, although not for long — awaiting Joe Root, he zigged towards a coach and a fielding drill, before zagging back to the centre.

How often these days is Smith alone? Of the captain of Australia, everyone wants a piece. Your life is planned to the smallest degree, your relationships defined by your role, your career at the beck of cricket's calendar. Perhaps the time Smith is closest to solitary is paradoxically when he is centre of attention, when he is at the crease, at one with his game, master of his skills.

Yesterday afternoon found him in that splendid isolation again, captain of Australia's fate as well as of its XI, his team four for 76 chasing 302. Another wicket would tilt the match decidedly England's way; Smith's wicket would have caused the visitors to surge to favouritism.

England had given his batting immense thought. They know his method front and back. Trevor Bayliss had the tyro Smith with New South Wales; his assistant Paul Farbrace coached Smith in the Kent 2nd XI. Previously they have favoured a fifth stump line to Smith, with catching strength; here the pitch was too slow. There was an old-fashioned point for Smith's diagonal back-foot slash; there were at various times a leg slip, a short mid-wicket, a short mid-on. The chief pressure, however, was the kind of Pareto principle of his team's top order, where Smith's minority input is almost invariably the majority output, and with Australian batting prospects seemingly as scarce as cabs round the Gabba.

Smith was 60 balls over his first 20, forty balls over his next 20, twenty-eight over the next 20 — moving, as they say, 'through the gears'. *Cricinfo* assessed his 'control' metric — an analytic that measures where strokes go relative to their intended direction — at better than 90 per cent throughout. 'Control' is not a word that springs immediately to mind watching Smith's herky-jerky fidgets and flexes, but the percentage brooked no argument.

Smith had hitherto experienced an in and out sort of season, and frankly so, conceding candidly six week ago that he 'wasn't holding the bat the way I like to' — something so basic and rudimentary that it seems likelier to befall a village hacker than captain of Australia, but somehow in keeping with the intuitive quality of his cricket.

Not geekily in thrall to technique, Smith eschews video to pick up his faults; he likes watching footage of himself making runs, for confidence's sake. When it feels wrong, he, in the modern parlance, 'finds a way'. It also fails to satisfy him. Chancing on a comfortable grip during the second Sheffield Shield round, he asked an umpire for tape in order to preserve it. It slipped, of course. But it was, perhaps, an early glimmer of the touch he has brought here. Two early on-drives for four from Broad went off with a crack like a Purdey discharging over a grouse moor.

In the last half hour, with thoughts of the morrow, Smith survived a canny spell from Anderson, who gave up a back-foot boundary, retaliated by beating his edge, and had him digging out his last delivery with a hasty jab. The third day will resume, at the improbably precise time of 9.58am, with further English shovelling required.

Before lunch, the tourists had belied their reputation as a team that bats deep by losing five wickets for 40, the first of them Dawid Malan, with a haphazard hook, the worst of them Chris Woakes, whose bat and front pad did not seem involved in the same match. Australia bowled short to useful effect, challenging hesitant horizontal bats, the expression 'tennis ball bounce' on this pitch being an insult to tennis balls.

In the field, however, England were quick on the uptake, supple and responsive. Smith's vice-captain, for example, was curbed by defensive fields and lengths. Warner responded thoughtfully, offering defensive shots and taking singles as a proclamation of serious intent. But the imp of the perverse in his make-up would not be denied, and his short-armed, cross-bat tug to short mid-wicket was an unnecessary indulgence.

Khawaja entered his contest with Moeen Ali, and with off-spin more generally, like a man entering a room full of rakes — it seemed only a matter of time before he stepped on one. He was lucky to last as long as two deliveries. The first ball turned past his sightless grope; the second, being only ten overs old, skidded into a dumbfounded pad. Khawaja did not even glance at his partner let alone a balcony, turning with a resigned sigh. He must find a way round those rakes.

The captain's other task during the 150-minute session after tea extended his role beyond that of soloist, to sympathetic accompaniest of Shaun

Marsh, who made batting appear both simplicity itself and every so often an accident waiting to happen, surviving a review, running sketchily. With such a strong example to draw on, Marsh unfolded fluently through the off-side in the final hour, and pleasingly for his captain. As serene a state as solitary excellence can be, Smith knows he will not regain the Ashes on his own.

BRISBANE TEST DAY 3

CUMMINS GOING

25 November 2017

At times in this decade, it has been difficult to sustain a belief in Patrick Cummins — not simply of his prowess, but almost of his very existence.

As a boom fast bowler, Cummins arrived with a heady rush, making his first-class debut in March 2011, barely a year after representing New South Wales under-17s, and his Test debut just six months later. He was hastily curtailed too, swallowed up by the infirmities of his teenage body. In the intervening years, witnesses against the Mafia have achieved greater visibility.

Cummins' solitary Test having been seen only on pay television, he left behind but meagre traces, barely stronger than rumours. He was genuinely quick, they reported. He was a potential matchwinner, they prophesied. All the king's horses and all the king's men were on the case, even if Humpty Dumpty was hardly an encouraging precedent. Nor was James Pattinson, contracted by Cricket Australia at the same time as Cummins, and seemingly on target to open the bowling with him in ... well, some day, in an unspecified future, blood, bone, tissues and humours permitting.

Pattinson's counter-example — he is now in search of a miracle surgery after four recurrences of stress fractures in his back — now provides a different context to Cummins' career. Even today, with all the resources and technology available to this wealthy game, we cannot always have nice things, especially fast nice things. Developing thoroughbred pace bowlers is as speculative an endeavour as breeding thoroughbred racehorses. Many are called, few chosen.

Though this has been his first Test in Australia and his first-class debut at the Gabba, it's impossible to describe Cummins in this match as a 'discovery' — he is the result of thousands of man hours and hundreds of thousands of dollars of clawing back, from points where he was proverbially Australia's best-paid student, taking a business degree at University of Technology Sydney as he inched along his road to recovery.

Yesterday was a part reflection of his interim priorities, the calm and competence of his 42 from 120 deliveries, outscoring his captain in a vital 69-run partnership, following from matches played at his grade club, Penrith, as a batsman only. He progressed, like his rehabilitation, by degrees: an authentic leg glance for four from Woakes, a fortunate five of overthrows from Ball, an insouciant slog sweep for six from Moeen tauntingly executed just after mid-on had been brought up.

On the first and second days, Cummins had bowled far faster than a standard first change bowler ought. Now he appeared better credentialed than a number nine batter — a drive on the up from Woakes almost justified his promotion to number six. After his captain brought up his century with a flourishing cover drive from Broad, Cummins reached his best Test score with a shot every bit as good from Anderson, puncturing point like a poison dart.

It was Steve Smith, of course, who delivered in expected manner, proceeding towards the match's first hundred and beyond almost by osmosis — a process natural, relentless, sometimes imperceptible but seemingly irreversible. Apparently unable to prevent it, England worked on delaying it by disruption, lures and ruses: packed off sides, packed on sides, overs in alternation from over and round the wicket.

As captain four years ago, Alastair Cook was criticised for chasing the game, while Michael Clarke sustained James Brown levels of funk. Yesterday Joe Root pushed for George Clinton status, at one stage posting twin leg side cordons half and seven-eighths of the way to the fence, premeditated enough to demand a neologism: the Yorkshire Wall, the Pennine Picket, the Brisbane Line etc. Smith met the challenge of inventiveness, at one stage fetching Woakes to leg from well above his eyeline with what resembled a two-fisted topspin forehand.

Smith could hardly have advanced so far, however, had Cummins and his tailend kinsmen not sold themselves so dearly. The tails may prove the tale of this Test: that England's last five first-innings wickets could eke out only 56, while Australia's last six wickets swelled their progress by 252. With their hosts seven for 209, the visitors would not have accounted for losing their highest Test runs scorer and highest first-innings scorer before erasing an arrears.

As the pitch fell into shadow, Cummins succeeded a rampant Mitchell Starc and bowled every bit as threateningly, the pitch having quickened up for three days of sun. Encircled by a leg slip, a short leg, a silly point and a hint of 2013-14, Root was alert, Mark Stoneman alarmed.

Cummins lacks as yet the full presence of a Johnson. His action is tightly grooved; his moustache looks scribbled on. But he does not turn twenty-five until May. A long time coming, Cummins could yet have a long time going.

METRIC CONVERSION

26 November 2017

Cricket loves metrics at the moment. No bit of data is too obscure or trivial to build a cult around. The Australians in the First Test, however, have at least one novel key performance indicator. As Josh Hazlewood revealed after the first day, they budgeted each day for one 'extraordinary moment' — an individual feat of particular dash and elan.

Hazlewood was speaking after Nathan Lyon's mercurial run out of James Vince, which assuredly qualified. David Warner's salmon-launching-up-a-stream catch of Jake Ball at short fine leg would have filled the quota on day two, while Mitchell Starc's limber snare of Alastair Cook at deep fine leg on day three was barely less meritorious.

Yesterday? The fall of Moeen Ali after lunch was not perhaps so extraordinary as opportunistically excellent. It was the Test's hottest, stickiest afternoon, after three days of unseasonal mildness. The batters had deposited a midden of gloves by the boundary's edge, nearby Tim Paine's spare gauntlets, both in token of the day's hard, close-quarters cut-and-thrust. The lulls in such cricket intensify the instants — time drifts by, then is lit by a flash.

Attempting to smother the second delivery of Lyon's nineteenth over, Moeen genuflected as low and far as physically possible, playing, missing and stretching. As his back toe dawdled in the vicinity of the line, Paine cuffed the bails, which ignited excitedly, and lit the trail to the third umpire's box.

It was not, perhaps, an especially difficult specimen of glovework. The delivery was visible all the way; it did not bounce or deviate untowardly; Peter Nevill and Matthew Wade would have backed themselves to execute it. But Paine is, narrowly and debatably, the man in possession, and in search of affirmations. Plus everyone loves a stumping: they are prized for their mousetrap-like springing, their scarcity and their strictness.

Cricket's applicable statute — Law 30.1.1 — demands that the batsman be 'considered to be out of his/her ground unless some part of his/her person or bat is grounded behind the popping crease'. In his little book *Cricket and Christianity*, the former Australian captain Brian Booth called this one of the moral lessons imparted by the cricket gods — it is not enough to be quite good; only the blameless life is truly virtuous.

To some observers here, however, this line exhibited a decided moral relativity. It was straighter than a river but bendier than a rod, and of a healthy width, more texta than ballpoint. A few, including Michael Clarke, detected molecules of Moeen in the safe zone; others took a more robust view, including, eventually, the only individual relevant, New Zealand's Chris Gaffaney. As a moment, it was assuredly of extraordinary significance, ending as it did England's chances of setting Australia a serious fourth-innings chase.

Tests, of course, are long and complex enough as not to depend on moments so much as phases. In this particular phase, either side of lunch, the ascendant belonged not to the keeper so much as the bowler. A year ago, Nathan Lyon kept his place in Australia's XI perhaps only because Steve O'Keefe twinged a hamstring in the Sheffield Shield. After an indifferent tour of Sri Lanka, and amid the explicit mandate for change, his tenure was as uncertain as at any stage since his emergence six years earlier.

Lyon is a cricketer attuned to the dressing room — it's why Mike Hussey bequeathed him the role of Australia's chief victory song chorister. His on-field travails bespoke a confusion and perplexity off it. Lyon's 2017 has been a leading indicator of growing collective confidence and purpose: his 51 wickets have come more frequently and cheaply than in any year of his career. He has gone beyond laying containing barrages to battering down walls. He has outbowled Moeen here by a margin widened by daylight, if excused a little by the Englishman's lack of overs coming into the match.

Lyon's dismissals of Stoneman and Malan before lunch were particular collector's pieces of off-spin to left-handers, drifting it in to the line of the stumps, kissing the edges on the way to Smith's meaty mitts at slip — catches the captain made look deceptively easy, to go with two others. There has hardly been a great batsman who was not also a great catcher.

Of the specialist batsmen that left Smith's counterpart, who had hardly played a false stroke in three hours. But with lunch warming in the bain-maries, Joe Root teetered to the off and was so lbw to Hazlewood that not even he could talk himself into a review. The ball's sharp jag may have been abetted by a crack; but the Australians, who have tended over time to bowl to Root either very full or very short, may have found a tincture of technical fallibility on which to concentrate for the rest of the series.

In the interim, Root has other worries. His schemes have steadily lost their novelty; his resources have looked ever shallower; his tallest scorer has had a barren Test; his five-man attack has punched at little better than half that weight; his team has won one and lost six of their last nine away Tests. England have done better here than some foresaw, without eliminating the notion that they are the combination in greater need of extraordinary moments.

BAIRSTOW AND BUTTHEAD

27 November 2017

Whenever representatives of England find themselves in adversity, one can expect parrot cries for Churchillian leadership. The trouble for its cricketers is that they've already had recourse to it. England's performance in the First Test recalls Earl Wavell's observation that his inspirational prime minister was always expecting you to pull rabbits from empty hats.

Joe Root did his best in Brisbane, and exhibited considerable personal grit. But circumstances have him waving a rather hollow topper. Nor is there much up his sleeve. Chris Woakes, for example, is a plucky cricketer, mainly in English conditions. Yet having him stand in as a pace bowling all-rounder for Ben Stokes is like casting Hugh Grant as Hannibal Lecter.

Through England's grim Saturday, when his team's condition deteriorated from queasy to gangrenous, Root must have wished for nothing more than an intervention by his team's number one match winner and scapegrace. One of Stokes' most valuable attributes with the ball is his versatility: he can swing it, angle it, bang it in, dry it up. In the field he exudes a presence both uplifting and intimidating. At the Gabba, Root was stuck with much the same and then more. He was alleged to enjoy the advantage of a fifth bowler, but Woakes and an underdone Jake Ball did not in the end total a single Patrick Cummins.

The strength in batting depth that England exhibited in their home summer, with Moeen Ali and Jonny Bairstow augmenting Stokes, was likewise missing. Moeen at six is not Moeen at eight; Bairstow was not his jack-in-the-box self. Late on the fourth day, it emerged that there may have been off-field reasons for this.

These may well have been 'blown out of all proportion', as Bairstow insists. But the proportion is inevitably distorted by it involving a cricketer already cautioned, after that night in Bristol, about his rackety nocturnal tendencies. That has thrown his own camp into needless confusion. Nobody associated with the England Cricket Board at yesterday's increasingly bizarre press conferences was at all sure what had happened except that nothing really had — one half expected to hear the headbutt explained as a traditional Yorkshire greeting. Whatever the case, there are grounds for considering Bairstow to have been reckless at least. Certainly, England can hardly afford another cricketer on the sidelines. *Hamlet* without the prince is bad enough; one would not wish it to proceed without Horatio and/or Fortinbras too.

All such developments go to relative confidence, and this was already in Australia's favour, with the abiding edge of their own conditions, crowds, meteorology, media, and in Brisbane so many powerful precedents. The hosts' record at the Gabba is so rich and consistent as to constitute its own genre. This match in some degree re-ran the First Test twenty-seven years ago, where three tightly-bunched innings climaxed with Australia streaking away by ten wickets. Stuart Broad's belief in England's 'perfect' position after day three was a quote of built-in obsolescence. 'For three days we played excellent cricket', as Root said yesterday, was as meaningless as a footballer patting themselves on the back for a well-organised corner.

Especially concerning for England is that as much went right for them as they could conceivably have expected, considering their gentle jog of preparation and indifferent results on tour. The toss went their way; the weather was kind; the pitch was two-paced, and quickened only gradually. The plans were thoughtful; the fielding was committed; the catching was spotless. Broad played above his recent form; James Anderson mostly maintained his. Above all, perhaps, given past experience, nobody was injured.

In these respects, then, Australia verifiably won the Test rather than England losing it, and suggested some resourcefulness in doing so. There was no scope for the 'Bodyline' melodramatically envisioned by the *Courier Mail*. On the contrary. They encountered a surface at the Gabba taking as much spin early as anyone could remember. Fortunately, they had the bowler of the match, Nathan Lyon, capable of taking advantage. They were, at times, kept waiting for wickets. Fortunately, they had the fielder of the match, also Nathan Lyon, capable of a crucial intervention against the run of play.

Steve Smith we knew about. It was as though England had budgeted for his hundred — they wished merely to put it off as long as possible. Lyon was a different matter. His excellent year had been spent largely overseas, on dusty wickets in hot countries during home football seasons. Australians awaited the evidence of their own eyes, and got it, both in the torque of his spin and the tourniquet of his control.

They heard it with their own ears too, Lyon leading into the game with some cheeky provocations — gratuitous, frankly, but he was given no reason to repent them. His confidence is gradually aligning with his record. This is also the kind of confidence a team can nourish when it understands its rivals to be at a clear handicap.

We will tire of saying it this summer, but it will be no less true for all that: Ashes Tests have not been so influenced by a cricketer's absence since Glenn McGrath tripped over his feet at Edgbaston in 2005 — which at least was an accident, far removed from tripping over one's fists. And so long as Stokes' bowling remains confined to social media, one fears that Root will be offering his blood, toil, tears and sweat without great cause for optimism.

ADELAIDE TEST DAY I

TOSS UP

2 December 2017

Captains who yield first innings on winning the toss are variously described. Sometimes they are said to have 'invited' their opponents to bat. Other times they are reported as having 'offered' their opponents 'first use'. Now and again, they 'elect to bowl', as though by ballot. Generically they are 'sending' the opposition in. In modern times, an additional thrust of strategic aggression is conveyed in the word 'insertion'.

Joe Root's decision in the Second Test at Adelaide Oval when the coin fell was categorically an insertion. Which is not to say that it would have been without misgivings. As the choice came his way, Root glanced furtively at the inconstant sky — probably more influential on his thinking than the coarse grass carpeting the dry surface. The meteorology recalled the cool mornings of the last Ashes so injurious to Australia, but with more bluster than an episode of *Q&A*.

Root would have been aware, too, that it is easier for a camel to thread the eye of a needle than to put the opposition in at the Adelaide Oval: only Clive Lloyd has done so successfully, and the West Indies' victory took a full fifteen sessions even with their team of the talents. But what price such analysis when Test cricket at night is so new, and the data sets are so limited? Some captain would have to be first inserter, as it were: it might, Root thought, as well be him.

It doubled as a gesture of overt enterprise. Leading in to the match, Root had promised an England galvanised and unified by Australia's barbed tongues, and the peals of Steve Smith's laughter. David Gower and Ian Botham talked Bob Willis into his ill-starred decision to bowl here thirty-five years ago — in that sense it was more of an 'invitation'. England's young captain owned this decision Root and branch.

Initially, England's was an insertion without push, the bowlers attacking the occasion rather than the stumps, leaving a pitch map that resembled a hail of buckshot. The stiff breeze did not help; the rain perversely did, providing the opportunity to take stock and recalibrate.

When play resumed at 4.45pm, after a second break, Anderson and Broad swapped ends to bowl to fuller and better effect, while Woakes winkled out a wasteful Warner. Three for 109 would have represented a healthy return on insertion had Mark Stoneman held Khawaja's top edge at long leg before dinner, even if it was not too costly a reprieve.

That left Steve Smith, which, these days, is a lot: he passed 3000 runs as captain, at an average trending towards 75. His defensive shots and check drives rifled off the bat; he got off the mark with a cover drive of lip-smacking perfection; he executed one leave with a signature chorus line kick. When, every so often, his edge was beaten, it seemed almost like an optical illusion.

Against Australia's captain, however, England were unmistakably more ambitious. Having challenged his patience in Brisbane, they here challenged his *sang froid*, Broad and Anderson taking charge of the repartee, as observers honed their distance lip reading skills. Smith showed willing, but did a sense of impunity kick in? Going more than ten and a half hours elapsed time between dismissals might do that to you. Whatever the case, the return of Craig Overton for a third spell seemed to induce a fatal relaxation. A nip-backer insinuated itself through a gate that was closed but not bolted.

That reopened Root's decision to debate: another wicket would have turned the insertion into an insurgency. Broad, who bowled manfully all day, tormented Peter Handscomb's outside edge, but could not defeat his inside edge. At times, the Australian's back-and-across step revealed two stumps behind him. But he concluded a year in Test cricket by steadily negotiating a solitary Anderson over with the second new ball.

The record crowd of 55,317 made it another fine advertisement for Test cricket's new variant and its fresh palette. In the afternoon, the day-night match resembled neither quite, the wan sun needing artificial help within a few overs of the start, and the light fluctuating like an expiring neon tube. The pink ball glowed, the players cast pale shadows and the illuminated signage flashed crescents of colour, even if no pinpoint was quite so bright as the old companion of the orange bulb by the striking batsman's name on the antique scoreboard.

The loveliest light of the day came after 6pm, by which time, of course, Test cricket has conventionally drawn stumps. But the fall of night after dinner revealed a brilliant tableau, the cricketers whiter and the grass greener for the 2500 lumens per square metre. The members gradually emptied in favour of the Village Green, but the Hill remained densely populated, and both sides could convince themselves of their day's share. But having sacrificed first innings, England must now bat last against the world's best off-spinner. The coin has fallen but keeps on rolling.

ADELAIDE TEST DAY 2

PAINE RELIEF

3 December 2017

'Whom the gods wish to destroy they first call promising.' Cyril Connolly's famous aphorism applies so readily to cricket it should almost be a motto — how readily the benediction becomes a burden. But let's be honest — it also has its advantages.

Tim Paine has been a promising cricketer since the middle of the last decade. He made his first-class debut so long ago it was in the Pura Cup. He made his Test debut when opponent Salman Butt was not associated with corruption and mendacity. The inflictor of an horrendous finger injury that threatened to ruin it all, Dirk Nannes, is comfortably established as a mild-mannered radio commentator.

There was consternation two weeks ago when Paine was recalled from the outskirts of the fringe of the hinterland of the wilderness of cricket to win his fourth Test cap more than seven years after his last. The advice from chairman of selectors Trevor Hohns was perplexingly worded: 'With Tim, it's been widely acknowledged for a small amount of time now that he is regarded as the best gloveman in the country.' How much width? How much smallness? It was widely acknowledged for a small amount of time that Hohns had taken leave of his senses.

But perhaps still more remarkable was that Paine was playing at all, with a record so thin, and a potential so vestigial. He has averaged 29 in first-class cricket over twelve years, and been for a good part of that period a keeping back-up in Tasmania, in recent times understudying the likes of Tom Triffitt and Jake Doran before this season slipping behind Matthew Wade.

So Paine's third Test half-century at Adelaide Oval yesterday, fully 2611 days after the second, was about more than a selectorial intuition. It was a testament to the resources of Australian cricket, financial, administrative and medical, that keeps players longer and better than any previous generation. On Friday Paine turns thirty-three, making him two years older than when Ian Chappell surrendered the Australian captaincy and four years older than when Garth McKenzie played his last Test. Not that long ago, a player with Paine's profile would hardly have lasted so long, and it was still a close-run thing: as Paine has disclosed, he had been busily exploring post-playing career options, convinced his time had run out. But his innings yesterday gave a glimpse of why he caught the eye in the first place.

At five for 209, with a ball just nine deliveries old, the match was if not at a tipping point at least approaching an incline, requiring resistance both stoic and enterprising. Shaun Marsh was providing the former, but it was Paine who struck the blue touchpaper against the friction of the hard Kookaburra.

A resounding pull and emboldened slash from James Anderson set him in motion; he drove Overton down the ground in the air with the same nonchalance as Brad Haddin four years ago. To approach his half-century, he hoisted the struggling Moeen well beyond mid-on; to sign it he slashed Overton over backward point with eye and nerve. In a trice, it seemed, Australia were advancing on 300, and England beating a disorderly retreat.

When Paine began his career, there was also no decision review system, which availed him at 24 when he was given out lbw. The only other setbacks were two blows to that right index finger, inflicted by Overton, after which one winced every time Paine touched gloves with his partner.

It has never been difficult to discern the watermark of quality in Paine's cricket — his athleticism, his compactness, his stroke production. The enigma, only partly explained by injury, is that record. Perhaps initial success and favour came too easily, too swiftly; perhaps, in that twilight between international and domestic cricket, he became neither one thing nor the other.

The lot of the wicketkeeper in Australia is unique. Only one can wear the baggy green at a time. The role was filled so superbly so long by Haddin, now Australia's fielding coach, that it ceased to be clear where Paine was headed. It's a wonder that more keepers do not lose heart at a glass ceiling with only one narrow trapdoor.

To return to Connolly's maxim, promise also mutates readily into cause for blame, internal as well as external. When you make it look easy, some will mark you harder. The short stuff continuing, Paine pulled Overton straight to Moeen at backward square leg — a muted ending to an innings worth far more than its weight in runs, and to a partnership with the whiff of Ashes about it.

Marsh, however, was now safely ensconced, and the cricket ball grew like a football in need of a bicycle pump. Without the atmospheric aid of the previous day, England's attack were badly exposed, with four variations on the same medium-paced theme, and a slow bowler going nowhere fast. Every now and again Marsh produced a stroke of princely quality; between times he could content himself with patient accumulation.

For Marsh, of course, promise has also been a blessing and an incubus, to the extent of a career batting in seven different slots, and involving eight separate comebacks. He has always had the capacity to touch peaks reserved for few, between plumbing valleys of mediocrity and timidity — this pinnacle concluded an excellent afternoon for Australian cricket. For England, the promise was altogether more menacing.

ADELAIDE TEST DAY 3

SCENIC ROOT

4 December 2017

'ENG WON TOSS.' Even the grand old Adelaide Oval scoreboard has
become a heckler here, enunciating the last two words of this information
with a golden yellow script in the bottom right hand corner. Joe Root would
have glimpsed it during his preparatory surveillances on emerging to bat
early yesterday afternoon. Can't even get the scorers off my case ....

Decisions like Root's have a way of following a captain round, acquiring
as they do a context from the unfolding of events. This is unfair, because
these subsequent events are complexly inflected. But the heads-or-tails
simplicity of the coin's fall offers immediate counterfactual possibilities.

Australia, of course, would have batted first regardless in this Second
Test: Steve Smith has said so. England might well have bowled as listlessly
in the first fifteen overs of their innings under those circumstances too. But
there is a developing sense of Root's choice as an expression of misgivings
about his task.

England arrived in Adelaide as motivated as could be, enjoined by Root
to remember Australia's taunts and guffaws of Brisbane, rallying loyally
round their slighted comrade Jonny Bairstow, lent an abrasive edge in the
field by a snarling and rasping Jimmy Anderson and Stuart Broad.

Yet as coach Trevor Bayliss explained in fronting the media on Sunday
evening, Root's forgoing of first innings for his batsmen was in search of
the 'best opportunity' for bowlers that are an abiding source of concern.
'It's well documented that one of our challenges is taking wickets on flatter
wickets,' Bayliss conceded. 'It's well documented they've got three guys who
are quicker than ours,' Bayliss conceded further. Presented with the relevant
documentation, Root was obliged to sign off on it.

When West Indies in 1982 became the only team to insert successfully,
Clive Lloyd swaggered into the field with Roberts, Holding, Garner and
Croft at his beck. Root sought to emulate him because he was mindful
of England's contrasting tour matches against the Cricket Australia XI:
pushing them over like dominoes with the pink ball here, bouncing off them
like a wall while using the red ball in Townsville.

It was not, then, a Hussain/Hutton howler. But it was a concession of
weakness rather than an assertion of strength. It imposed an onus on the
bowlers on the first two days to which they proved unequal, and a penalty on

the batsmen on the third day of which they could hardly have been unaware. Not that the surface has deteriorated — if anything, barely blemished, it has sped up a little. But none for 0 is an altogether more solemn undertaking when it comes in the wake of eight declared for 442, instead of following a successful call and confident appropriation of first innings: one is in constant danger of falling between stools, of keeping the target in mind or deliberately expelling it from the same. Which is pretty much where Root fell yesterday facing his tenth ball, knocking over both stools, an occasional table and an expensive lamp by driving expansively at Patrick Cummins.

So it continued, as Australia bowled with the kind of precision and discipline that preys on conglomerated minds — batsmen not sure if they were attacking or defending, striving or surviving. Vince, Moeen and Bairstow fell to attempted scoring strokes that called for defence; Cook defended what he might have left alone. Nobody, strictly speaking, played a culpable shot; nor, until the tenacious eighth-wicket pair of Woakes and Overton, did anyone suggest permanence.

The salient wicket was Cook after a two-hour vigil, four years on from being immolated here by Mitchell Johnson. Now he perished with surprising gentleness, poking needlessly at an off-break. Lyon has now dismissed England's tallest Test scorer six times, more than any current Australian bowler — a useful ascendancy to enjoy. Here was not, then, so much a collapse as a steady subsidence or controlled demolition, around the structural weakness of England's desire to accommodate a fifth bowler — more to the point, a fifth bowler who is not Ben Stokes.

This has already had some peculiar public outcomes. A few months ago in England, for example, Bayliss found himself explaining why Moeen Ali was the team's 'second spinner' at a time there was not actually a first. 'Mo is a bit of a complex character at times,' said the coach, as if describing Holden Caulfield. But there must also be a sort of cumulative psychic toll, on bowlers aware they are not quite good enough, on batsmen conscious that they bear an individually greater burden because of those limitations. 'They're confident,' Bayliss insisted of his charges on Sunday night. 'There's a good feeling in the dressing room.' But here there's also a touch of Holden, who famously never knew what he was going to do until he did it.

England's cause might have been lost altogether but for Steve Smith's reticence about the follow-on, which if ever an option was so last evening. A new ball and twenty-nine overs under lights looked an enticing assignment, but the tyranny of bowling 'loads', one presumes, exercised its dominion. When Australia elected to bat again, England, with no necessity to spread the work, and no particular burden of expectation, were able to inflict some late casualties. For a captain whose opponent was 268 ahead with six wickets in hand, Root walked off in a merry mood — merrier, certainly, than he had departed earlier. But it is respite rather than redemption.

SIGNS OF A CONTEST

5 December 2017

It has been a big, buoyant, noisy, crowded Test match at Adelaide Oval, with attendance records smashed, a party atmosphere on the Village Green and ample Barmy Army bonhomie. But as dinner neared yesterday, the stands and hills were disarmingly quiet.

An improbable chase was taking shape. Challenging deliveries were eliciting subdued gasps. Tidy overs were occasioning ripples of applause. A visiting journalist in the press box had recourse to Michael Frayn's line, that the despair he could handle, it was the hope he couldn't stand.

England had come to Adelaide Oval thinking that it might be their best chance on tour, thanks to the caprices of the pink ball under lights. Little in the Test's first eight sessions had encouraged that view. They had sent Australia in, squandered two new balls, wasted a succession of starts, conceded the tallest total in day-night Tests and incurred a first-innings deficit of 215.

Trail so far and so long in any other form of sport and there would be no chance of coming back; there was barely a chance here. But now Steve Smith was standing at slip wondering if he had made one. Spared the follow-on, in order that Smith might slightly spare his bowlers, England were about 300 runs from equalising a series in which they have struggled all the way to keep up.

Suddenly, in fact, the series looked rather like what it is on the rankings tables: a middling clash, third versus fifth, featuring two honest but fallible teams whose best cricketers would form an excellent combined XI. Not that there's anything wrong with that — in fact it can make for entirely absorbing cricket, rivals striving to make good their limitations and to extend their capacities.

England have by far the tougher task in these Ashes, a long way from home comforts, not as far but far enough from their best cricketer. And there was just a hint in Smith's decision to bat again in the third innings that he was acting on that reasoning, contemplating the Third Test before completing the Second. But if there was a desire to weary England's bowlers with several long sessions in the field, and to delay England's batting in the fourth innings until night closed in, the Australians had a funny way of showing it. Despite commencing the day at a rather bedraggled four for 54, the hosts' batting had a demob happy aspect. Peter Handscomb was impatient and Shaun Marsh overambitious, offering crooked bats at shaping deliveries. Nathan Lyon ended his nightwatch with a flamboyant away step. Tim Paine and Mitchell Starc holed out in the deep, while Patrick Cummins tried to. The depth of the tourists' attack, overtaxed in the first innings, was this time untested: Moeen Ali had to provide a mere five overs, Craig Overton only two one-over spells.

England, by contrast, bustled purposefully, with the incentive that they could leave it no later. James Anderson would simply not be denied, bowling nineteen of the first forty-two overs at untiring pace, gliding through the crease like an apparatus of swivels and pulleys, culminating in an almost audible snap as the fingers discharged the ball. Chris Woakes seized on the pink ball as he had here three weeks ago; Dawid Malan accepted a sharp chance at third slip; Overton scooped an awkward catch at long leg. When Starc turned Moeen round the corner, Jonny Bairstow hared off from behind the stumps, shedding his helmet and right glove as he chased three-quarters of the way to the boundary; later he scooted after a top-edged hook from Cummins, and relayed a powerful return. Had England spoken with their actions like this from Saturday, their victory target would have been nothing like the eventual 354.

As England commenced this pursuit, the Australians sought to reassert themselves. Starc followed through with a trail of asperities. Lyon edged in from point to reconnoitre the crease with a proprietorial air. Mark Stoneman replied with three consecutive leg-side boundaries as Starc strained for the lethal length he hit in the first innings; three further boundaries followed in Josh Hazlewood's fourth over. In that way of cricket when the trend is running, England also began accruing the breaks.

Early on, Hazlewood slammed an inducker from round the wicket into Alastair Cook's back pad. It appeared to the naked eye to be making its way peacefully past leg stump: certainly Cook affected unconcern, looking down at his crease and lightly marking his guard, as unself-conscious as a man brushing lint from his trousers. The appeal came early enough in the innings that Smith thriftily decided against a review; ball tracker suggested it would have been a wise investment. If DRS is to be believed, in fact, the naked eye has had a bad Test match.

Redress took a further hour and a half, Smith electing, not without hesitation, to review Lyon's impact on Cook's front pad. But after dinner, Australia's captain, who has no face for poker, could be observed in a Simon Says of hands on hips and hands on heads. Twice in three balls he tried his luck, a little desperately, with the DRS, to no avail.

The crowd had by now recovered its partisan voice. English fans received the review verdicts with gleeful abandon; Australians roared when Cummins stuck a retaliatory shiv through Malan's forward prod. So a Test that has not so much ebbed and flowed as veered and wobbled approached its final day — a Test that Michael Frayn would have loved, even as he hated it.

SMILES AND GRIMACES

6 December 2017

As the crowd dispersed at Adelaide Oval yesterday afternoon, Steve Smith appeared on the video screen at the cathedral end, rigid and square-shouldered, rictus stretched across his face. He thanked us for our custom, hoped we had enjoyed our experience, and to see us again soon, all the whole while looking like his preference would have been for extensive dental work.

About half an hour after the fall of the last wicket, having submitted patiently to his losers' media conference, Joe Root could be seen moving patiently along the boundary in front of the Riverbank Stand shaking hands, signing autographs and posing for selfies, even doing the job himself with the iPhones and iPads proffered by their owners. His smile was not so much excruciated as automated, as grooved as a drive at a throwdown.

Who would be a captain? Perhaps in international cricket only the decisions of the umpire are so closely scrutinised, and these are only subject to technological review. The captain is up for non-stop rolling scrutiny of a jury heavily weighted with … well, with former captains. Not to mention myriad armchair strategists on whose speculations nothing hinge.

Censure can even develop a moral tone. Too attacking and they are naïve. Too defensive and they are pusillanimous. They are nominally in charge in a game full of randomness and chance. They carry the can for others' every failing and folly. Few Tests have borne this out as faithfully as the Second at Adelaide Oval.

In financial markets, the expression 'Texas hedge' is applied to a strategy to minimise risk that results in its exacerbation. It did not apply exactly to the contested choices made by Joe Root and Steve Smith in the last five days — in each case to bowl or not to bowl — but both were undoubtedly hedges. Root sought precautions against the limitations of his thinly-stretched five-man attack on flat pitches. Smith wished to guarantee against excessive strain on his hard-working four-man attack over the course of summer.

Neither could be said to have borne fruit: England conceded eight for 442 when they bowled first; Australia folded for 138 when they eschewed the follow-on. Yet in neither case were the captains wholly blameworthy. Root was hardly responsible for England's dilatory bowling on the first day; Smith could do little from the dressing room to address Australia's haphazard batting on the fourth. Intermittent rain and unseasonal mildness played a part; likewise the pink ball's unpredictable humours.

Above all, their captaincy calls this season are being dictated by personnel. Root has been deprived of his team's all-round fulcrum; Smith is aware that his bench strength is thinning. They must cut their captain's blazers according to their team cloth. Neither has a great combination, having lost Tests to West Indies and Bangladesh respectively in the last few months.

In the end, England left themselves too much to do on the final day here. There are sound reasons that nobody has chased more than 315 to win at Adelaide Oval in 140 years. Even in this age of tarmac-like drop-in pitches, the weight of precedent bears down on players. In a fourth innings errors are more obviously culpable and meaningful; you need luck, and that can never be assumed.

Smith came away from events with a mix of relief and chagrin, left to own his follow-on decision by both assistant coach Saker and strike bowler Starc, and admitting it had cost him sleep. His eventual dreams were probably haunted by hot spots and ball trackers; he'd have ordered cautiously at the breakfast buffet.

In the nearer term, however, each captain faces a great and underacknowledged challenge, which is to maintain their own individual performance standards over the next three Tests. Neither man is obtaining strong support from their batting colleagues; both might need to do a little more bowling; the fans expect.

Root has toiled over his technique since Brisbane, where he was twice snagged on the crease lbw. Facing Cummins early on in his second innings, he jabbed down late on a swift delivery angled into his pads, and formed his gloves right hand into a fist, remonstrating with himself. He nicked off yesterday also coming down late, having let the previous ball go, perhaps allowing discipline to get the better of him.

Smith, having basked in the Brisbane sun, was discomfited under Adelaide lights, pinned down and nagged out in the first innings, tackled from round the wicket in the second. Anderson worked over his defence like a bank robber seeking a safe's combination; their encounter in Perth looms large.

Captains become so because they are outstanding cricketers. Their additional leadership tasks then complicate the maintenance of those standards, even as nothing enriches their standing quite so much as individual performances. This makes Smith's average of 70 as captain all the more astonishing; Root's average of 54 as captain likewise attests his toughness. But they are marked men in this series for that very reason, opponents vying to wipe off their smiles.

ADELAIDE TEST REVIEWED

FOUR OF A KIND

8 December 2017

Can anyone or anything, strictly speaking, ever 'live up to the hype'? It is, after all, hype — and hyperbole, by definition, consists of 'exaggerated claims not meant to be taken literally'. Becoming literal, these cease to be hype. QED.

Pardon the pedantry: its relevance lies in reviewing the success in the first two Tests of Australia's three-prong pace attack, Mitchell Starc, Josh Hazlewood and Patrick Cummins. Before the series, they were heavily hyped. Ryan Harris even thought them the superior of the trio he formed four years earlier with Mitchell Johnson and Peter Siddle. Glenn McGrath anointed Starc 'the best bowler in the world'; his captain called him an 'absolute genius'; a video of him bouncing Usman Khawaja in the nets circulated like the work of a Russian electoral hacker. Cryptocurrencies have changed hands at fairer value.

In fact, Starc, Hazlewood and Cummins have not had it all their own way since, being held at bay on the first day of the series, being checked under lights, at times searching a little hard for swing, at other times maybe straining for pace. But now, let it be said, they're starting to click, in wickets and knots. The statistics tell a tale: Starc has 14 wickets at 18.7, Cummins and Hazlewood seven wickets each at 27.7 and 29.7 respectively. The last day at Adelaide Oval dawned brightly for England, whose strength had hitherto been said to lie in their lower-middle echelons. In fact, the visitors lost seven for 64 in 147 deliveries — a testament to both lethality and parsimony.

For England, the conditions in Adelaide were meant to represent their greatest opportunity of summer — pink ball, artificial illumination, benign weather. But what's sauce for the goose, eh? When Starc bowled the first over of England's reply, he wound the dial up on speed so effortlessly that it was almost like watching the main event after a curtain raiser. The first ball of his first over was the fastest of the match, at 146kmh; then so was the last ball of his first over, breaking through 150kmh, and stirring a sonic boom of appreciation from the crowd, some of whom might have cast their mind back to four years earlier when another Mitch was sustaining similar velocities.

How to deploy such resources? Skipper Smith is still learning. In Adelaide it coloured his captaincy. Scorning to enforce the follow-on was all about easing his precious pace bowlers' workloads and sparing them until after darkness's fall, even if his batsmen did not receive the memo, and lasted only 58 overs; Smith also remains surprisingly slow to post short catchers to leg, behind and in front of square. The trio did the job on the fifth day anyway, Hazlewood breaking the game open, Starc closing the game out, and Cummins excellent throughout.

In fact, for all that he has taken half as many series wickets as Starc and has played a fifth as many Tests as Hazlewood, it has been Cummins who has really impressed this summer, with spells of unremitting economy, allowing fewer than 2.5 an over in his auxiliary role, and unflagging speed, routinely clocking in the high 140s. When he hit tailender Craig Overton on the last day, it seemed for a moment like the ball would have to be pulled out from between the young Englishman's ribs.

Above all, Cummins has demonstrated a striking maturity for a player who has played only ten first-class matches other than his seven Tests. He understands game moments: as Australia zeroed in on victory on Wednesday, for example, he concluded an over to Jonny Bairstow with a bouncer so that Starc could have his chance at Stuart Broad, gratefully accepted. He contributes above and beyond: his partnerships of 66 with Smith in Brisbane and of 99 with Marsh in Adelaide have been integral to Australia's building first innings scores beyond their rivals. Having been a showcase for Australia's strength and conditioning capacities over the preceding five years, Cummins has this year proven a fine advertisement for its high-performance group, its coaches and selectors.

What is really making the configuration work, however, is Nathan Lyon, whose 109 overs have cost only 2.29 runs each, yielded eleven wickets at 22.7, but just as importantly afforded opportunities for the pace trio to regain their wind and return refreshed. On a slow wicket in Brisbane, Lyon was a patient foil for his faster teammates; in Adelaide, he showed hometown nous.

Lyon's English counterpart Moeen Ali, by contrast, has been able to get through 63 overs for two wickets, leaving Joe Root with no choice but to turn back to James Anderson again and again. England will now surely be worried about Anderson's 35-year-old physique, particularly if he wants to continue bowling round the wicket — which is how he strained his side and missed the last two and a half Ashes Tests of 2015.

Attacks cannot operate at one pace alone. Even in the summer of 1974-75, synonymous with the speed of Dennis Lillee and Jeff Thomson, more Australian overs were delivered by medium-pacer Max Walker and the slow bowlers Ashley Mallett and Terry Jenner, while part-timers Doug Walters and Ian Chappell provided in excess of 100 deliveries per Test. It is one thing to have a hot attack; quite another to make it work. Assuming it is possible to live up to hype, it can surely never happen without help.

THE DUCKETT AFFAIR
BEN 2
11 December 2017

It was never going to require much for this England team to go
from a state of slight smouldering to the appearance of a full-fledged
dumpster fire. There was too much fuel lying round; too many potential
combustions; too many observers, perhaps, unconsciously willing it on.
All it took was the combined influence of two Bens, neither of whom will
feature in the Ashes, for Australians to be dissolved into fits of laughter.

They shouldn't be too smug. Just over two years ago it was Australia's
turn to look a shambles. The captain could not buy a run; nor, in due
course, could the team. Two fine cricketers, Brad Haddin and Shane
Watson, were jettisoned. There was much binding in the Marshes. Seldom
has an Australian team looked as directionless and, frankly, disconsolate.

Look back a little further to the twin Ashes of 2013-14, and both teams
exhibited tendencies towards chaos. Warner in the Walkabout loosened the
wheel nuts on Australia; the collapsing form of Graeme Swann, Matt Prior,
Kevin Pietersen et al then blew the chassis off England. Coaches of both
countries lost their jobs; so, in due course, did the England team director
Paul Downton.

No beaten team is happy. But at least as fascinating as anything on
the field in this decade's Ashes has been the rivals' sheer brittleness, their
propensities to dominate and to capitulate, and the recourse to scrutiny of
'culture' — that popular two-dollar word for what used to be called 'team
spirit'. Strange, really, as there have surely never been more managers,
support staff, security personnel, communications officers and external
consultants involved in the running of their tours. Or maybe not so strange
at all.

Like Cricket Australia, the England Cricket Board is a sizeable business
with a considerable remit. It is, this summer, running three teams in
Australia — not just a Test squad, led by Joe Root, but an England Lions, led
by Keaton Jennings, followed in due course by a one-day party, led by Eoin
Morgan.

I use the word 'led', but this is virtually an archaism. While the captains
take charge on the field, they are integrated with a leadership structure
involving Trevor Bayliss and Andy Flower, itself answerable to Downton's
successor Andrew Strauss, who reports in to ECB chief executive Tom

Harrison and his chairman Colin Graves. Competent and knowledgeable men, no doubt. But because responsibility in this structure is diffuse, impressions of confusion are seldom far to seek.

Witness Brisbane. Confronted with the molehill of Jonny Bairstow's headbutt, England heaped up a well-meaning mountain, first parading the hapless Bairstow, who was constrained from answering questions, next the bemused Bayliss, who was restricted in answering questions by his lack of information, next the perplexed Root, baffled to be fielding questions about a three-week-old triviality rather than a half-hour old Test defeat, and finally Strauss, followed inevitably up the chain of command.

The result was a message, to say the least, mixed — that an 'incident' hardly worth the name could only be addressed by a curfew that nobody wanted, none benefited from and yet was regarded as inevitable because management had to be seen to be doing something.

The reason for this, of course, was Ben Stokes. One infraction is an incident, two a trend. Ironically, I suspect that the matters of Stokes and Bairstow are distantly related despite their hugely discrepant significance. A night out in a pub after arriving would have looked a relaxingly familiar way for England's cricketers to demonstrate that they weren't spooked by events in Bristol in September. It probably seemed a good idea to have the senior and junior squads mingle on Thursday night too. And if it was tone deaf to send them back to the same Perth hostelry as before, then maybe this was another lunge for normality, for release. Then ... well ... Ben Duckett, who will have frequent flier miles alone to show for his visit to Australia, as well as a big 'Please Sledge Me' sign on his back henceforward.

Again, though, this story evolved bizarrely, apparently from a report by the team's own security detail, even if what it had to do with security one can hardly tell, unless the threat to James Anderson's head has been graded 'critical' by MI5. Again, luckless Bayliss found himself in a position which few coaches would relish, stuck with minimising Duckett's as a foolish act of youthful high spirits ('a trivial thing'; 'small problems') yet obliged to treat it with the utmost gravity ('it doesn't matter how trivial it is'; 'some guys have to pull their head in').

Duckett, in due course, received similar treatment from the ECB as Sam Dastyari got from Bill Shorten when he was 'very, very strongly counselled', and a swingeing fine and suspension preluded a further outbreak of chin-stroking. A further line of communication was opened up by Anderson. 'A bit of a non-event'; 'a pretty silly incident'; 'an unfair question mark over our culture': his column in London's *Telegraph* sounded a wounded note on his own and his colleagues' behalf. On which Root was compelled to comment, his concession of a 'little bit' of disappointment with Anderson being likewise extensively parsed.

Alastair Cook put the tour into a loyally sober perspective on Tuesday. Perhaps, he conceded, the team had been slow to realize that the world had 'obviously changed' since that fateful night in Bristol; they had not, however, stinted on effort. 'I've never seen a team work as hard as this side is working,' he insisted, to the extent that players 'desperate to do well' were having to be held back by coaching staff.

It's also possible that the change is more general: that touring has grown so complex and hectic, teams so diverse and temporary, management so pervasive and hypervigilant, mainstream media so inquisitive and social media so instant that risk is ingrained in the system. In which case talk of the 'culture' is maybe half-right, in that it is formed by external as well as internal forces.

CRICKET HEREDITY

RUNS IN THE FAMILY

12 December 2017

The love of cricket is contagious but also hereditary, and when communicated in the blood can take on history-making qualities.

In the 1980s, Geoff Marsh, Chris Broad and David Bairstow were accomplished cricketers for Australia and England. On Thursday it may be that four of their sons take the field: Geoff's offspring Shaun and Mitchell for Australia versus Chris's son Stuart and David Bairstow's son Jonny. In 140 years of Test cricket, patrimony has never been such an exhibit.

Watching Australia and England this summer has already had a somewhat nostalgic temper. Forty years ago, Chris Broad and Geoff Marsh played under-19 cricket against one another; ten years later they made Ashes centuries opening the batting for their respective countries. To see Stuart, a sleeker version of Chris, bowl to tall, lean, left-handed Shaun, who looks like right-handed Geoff in the mirror, is to be reminded that the Ashes are fertile soil for rivalry.

Watching Jonny Bairstow behind the stumps, meanwhile, I recall a boyhood night at the SCG watching bonny David Bairstow helping to win a low-scoring one-day international for England. 'We can piss this,' said Bairstow when joined by his Yorkshire teammate Graham Stevenson at eight for 129 chasing 163. *Wisden* called the long-serving gloveman as 'perhaps the only unequivocally popular man in Yorkshire.'

Sporting fathers and sons are hardly so unusual, of course. Australian football rejoices in names like Ablett, Silvagni, Shaw and Watson, Australian rugby league in the families Hughes, Pearce, Rogers and Morris. Many pursuits have legendary examples of filial piety: association football's Bruces, Cruyffs and Redknapps, baseball's Gwynns and Griffeys, hockey's Hulls, basketball's Bryants.

Yet not all sports reproduce lineally. Only four father-and-son pairs have cracked tennis's top 100 in the half-century of the open era. Sons have struggled to measure up to famous fathers in golf. Who remembers Gary Nicklaus or Kevin Stadler? And cricket as a family affair has a particularly strong provenance. The first master cricketer, W. G. Grace, was part of a mighty brotherhood from Gloucestershire's Downend — the same vicinity as the family Broad, as it happens. Donald Bradman was inducted in the game by a maternal uncle who captained Bowral Town CC, the Chappells by a grade cricketer father and Test cricketer grandfather: the English title of Ian's autobiography *Chappelli* (1976) was *Cricket in our Blood*.

Scyld Berry provided empirical verification of the significance of family ties to the sport in his *Cricket: The Game of Life* (2016): he reported that a quarter of those who have represented England have had a father, brother or uncle who did the same; a further sixth had a first-class cricketer as father, brother or half-brother. Jonny Bairstow meets both criteria: his half-brother Andrew played for Derbyshire. Success, of course, is never guaranteed. To some careers there have developed rough parallels: Jeff and Simon Jones were both fast bowlers whose careers were curtailed by injury in their mid-twenties.

Survey Australian domestic cricket ranks at the moment and there is a goodly supply of familiar names: Harper, Moody, O'Donnell, Stobo and, of course, Lehmann, Jake when he was nine experiencing a Test where his father Darren was playing for Australia and his uncle Craig White playing for England. Tasmania's squad features no fewer than four sons of first-class cricketers. The last two of Alex Doolan, James Faulkner, Nick Buchanan and Ben McDermott also had brothers who played Sheffield Shield. We are beginning at last to see the emergence of daughters as well as sons: Queensland boasts Georgia Prestwidge, daughter of Scott and brother of Jack, and Jemma Barsby, daughter of Trevor and brother of Corey. Not to forget Will and Annabel Sutherland, who might outstrip their father James' representative honours with Victoria if probably not his administrative laurels with Cricket Australia.

What underlies this nature of cricket as a family game? Genetic inheritance obviously; doubtless also brand recognition, a recognisable surname, acting as a kind of quality certification, being no handicap to advancement. But cricket is also a time-consuming activity whose training accents technique, repetition and volume, and a punishing game richly sewn with failure. To both these a strong paternal bond can provide support and succour. Nor should access to facilities be underestimated. Geoff Marsh himself benefited from his father Ted laying a pitch and investing in a bowling machine at the family's sheep farm in Wandering. Shaun then had a bowling machine too: Mitch.

Jonny Bairstow presents perhaps the most intriguing case study. He became the thirteenth English Test cricketer with a Test cricketer father five years ago and, as he notes in his deeply moving autobiography *A Clear Blue Sky* (2017), 'the only son whose dad wasn't there to see him play', David having taken his own life in 1998. Long before Jonny played Ashes cricket, he had seen his father's ashes scattered at his favourite cricket ground, picturesque Scarborough, whose memorial garden features a commemorative plaque.

As Jonny remembers of his 8-year-old self: 'With my dad gone, I made a resolution to myself. I would become the man of the house.' His mother Janet recalls him saying: 'Don't worry Mum, we're going to be all right.' He pursued a sporting career determinedly, almost, one feels, as an act of homage. Certainly he has never ducked comparison with his father: sharing David's ginger hair, he even came to share his nickname, 'Bluey'.

The fifth of January 2018 will mark two decades since the tragic death of the original 'Bluey'. New model 'Bluey' will mark it by participating in a Test match on the ground where his father boldly predicted pissing a win against the Aussies. He is a brave cricketer who has done it the hard way, and shown the love of the game to be perdurable.

PACE LIKE FIRE

14 December 2017

'None of us like it. It's just that some of us show it more than others.' As a batsman's view of extremely hostile fast bowling, the old line of England's Maurice Leyland has remained hard to improve on. It is a test of mettle and nerve; it is also a test of the capacity to front up with unchanged demeanour to the next delivery when the last has not yet left your mind.

This was England's task at the WACA yesterday, to give ground where necessary without giving way, in the face of three fast bowlers in the pink of form. Specifically it was Mark Stoneman's about twenty minutes after lunch when he faced Josh Hazlewood's twelfth over.

For years, the WACA's residual reputation for pace and bounce has been something fashionable to mourn, like the quality of *The Simpsons* and/ or *Star Wars*, or like Malcolm Turnbull's residual liberalism. Yesterday, at perhaps the last opportunity, they made a reappearance, the ball threatening splices and sternums, bat-pads and gullies loitering with intent.

Early on, the Australians perhaps leaned against their instincts, trying calmly to ration the short ball and chiefly to menace the stumps, which ensured a steady supply of deliveries to be worked to leg and punched down the ground, although also two lots of four byes that Tim Paine could only have reached atop a human pyramid. England jog-trotted through the first hour at a run-a-minute — a quaint old measure these days, if in keeping with the WACA's 1980s décor. Cummins' first ball after lunch seemed to prelude a change of policy, even if it cleared Joe Root by the batsman's height again.

Gradually, Australia's pace trio hit lengths more systematically dangerous, and challenged the Englishmen to work their way out, with the bouncer deployed in an offensive capacity, rather than as a surprise, a variation or as a feint preluding a fuller ball. As Hazlewood took the ball from the Lillee-Marsh Stand End, Stoneman had just reached his third Test fifty with an insouciant slash over slips; he had also just been dropped, his outside edge taking so long to reach Mitchell Marsh at a deep-set first slip that thought clouded reflex.

There was a short leg for the fend, a deep backward square for the pull, two gullies for the cut. They were, at first, unneeded. Hazlewood's first delivery, arrowing in from round the wicket, hit Stoneman's so hard it warranted calling Air Crash Investigators. The helmet reeled. Bits flew. Stoneman's head would have rung like the bells of St Clement's. He did not drop; he walked to on side, shaken, as if by bad news. One wondered immediately — spectators, teammates, opponents — how bad it might be. Support staff dashed from the bench to check, with a battery of tests for concussion; Stoneman uneasily palped his jaw.

Hazlewood pondered his next move alone at the end of his mark, and more or less knew what it had to be. This time Stoneman raised his gloves self-protectingly, and a chance looped toward an on-rushing Lyon at the squarer gully, dislodging as he hit the ground. How much Stoneman saw of the next four balls, only he can say, but outwardly he withstood the test. He has looked the part this summer, without perhaps having the runs to show for it. He is neither hasty nor languid: he awaits bowlers as they turn, sometimes stooping over his bat when they are halfway on their walkback, projecting a willing readiness. There was now one play and miss, but also a decisive duck, while Hazelwood's two full deliveries were recognised and safely parried.

You need good fortune to outlast such conditions, and England perhaps lacked it. Root feathered an edge down the leg side — a muted end in such a red-blooded contest. Stoneman was reviewed out on suspicion of a hemi-demi-feather of a glove — a ruling made by third umpire Aleem Dar with surprising alacrity. Both batsmen looked suitably desperate. That ancient riff about the WACA's speed comes with the rider that it is among the best places in the world to bat, pace onto the bat making for pace leaving it, a frictionless outfield offering value for shots. Once in, it is well worth staying.

Stoneman had, however, done his job, soaking up the best of Hazlewood, allowing scope for greater later enterprise, some of which recalled the WACA's palmy days. Dawid Malan's gritty half-century included a six hooked almost as fine as Roy Fredericks' famous blow here in 1975. The batsmen were enjoined to positivity from the commentary box by Geoffrey Boycott, who forty years ago spent a day here scoring 63. The WACA itself was a picture — stands full, grassed expanses welcoming, signage heavy on the green beneath the cloudless azure blue sky, while the Optus Stadium bulked in the distance like an alien starship.

The present impinged on the news front, with all the talk of the morning being of *The Sun*'s spot-fixing scoop by an aspiring Wenlock Jakes. This led to lots of solemn television discussion about the evils of betting with a backdrop of bet365 hoardings and leading into a Ladbroke's advertisement. Word also wafted from New Zealand that Ben Stokes had hit his straps for

Canterbury — an event of ever diminishing relevance as the series passes its half-way point. Had Stokes only punched Mr Big and The Silent Man, he might now be a hero ....

In fact, England looked less like needing their star all-rounder today than in any day on tour, Jonny Bairstow looking a more natural fit at number six than Moeen Ali. It remained hard graft as they pressed on after tea, but they continued not to show the strain.

WARNER AT BAY

15 December 2017

In the Perth Test match four years ago here, both Steve Smith and David Warner scored hard-driving hundreds, flattening England then reversing over them. The visitors have returned to Australia with plans for both. They are working roughly as well as plans do.

The WACA, where he arrived with a Test average of 89 and strike rate of 90, has become something of a playpen for Warner — he will miss its bounce and carry as much as any fast bowler. So England persevered yesterday, as it has all summer, with a policy of austerity. Australia's pace attack had posted extra gullies, short legs, leg slips. Showing up as 10-15kmh slower than their counterparts, England approached Warner straight, with three on the one side, James Anderson from over the wicket with a backward point 30m from the bat, Broad from round the wicket with a backward point on the fence.

Warner can handle this, and well. In Chittagong in September, he toiled a day over 123, hitting only seven boundaries, as Mushfiqur Raham elected to patrol the perimeters rather than crowd him up close. Warner recognised the intended affront to his 'ego', and rather enjoyed the novelty of his hundred's drawing out.

Yet the question arises how far Warner wants to carry such patience in Australia. Commentators here rise an octave when he is on strike; spectators reach, as it were, for the popcorn. Watching Warner merely accumulate is like watching a big-name star try to make their way through a crowd without being recognised. It feels different; it *is* different. Six years ago at this ground, Warner blasted a hundred in a pyrotechnic session against India, starting with a half-century in 36 deliveries; yesterday in that time he cuffed and dabbed ten singles.

Between times emerged hints of a wandering mind: he essayed an uppercut and missed; he prodded at a ball he might have left. Overton's next delivery, angled in, was officially measured jagging 1.5 degrees as Warner went at it, hard-handed and flat-footed, heading off with a fist clench of annoyance. As batting by Warner goes, it was like borrowed clothing — somehow not belonging.

Overton carried on effectually, trapping Bancroft, almost accepting a difficult return catch from Usman Khawaja, almost unsettling Steve Smith with a sudden lifter on the stroke of tea. After tea, however, Smith made light of Australia's task. England's plans for him this summer, further restricted here by little swing, have availed them little.

The WACA's bounce brings out Smith's powerful right hand, honed in junior tennis — it still makes shapes like a forehand. Broad thought to bounce him above the eyeline: Smith hooked it into the gold seating at fine leg, hot spot revealing a bulls' eye in the middle of the bat. Broad followed up with a delivery into the ribs: Smith's retort was not a hook, or a pull, but a whisk through mid-wicket, executed slightly off balance, but hit so hard that nobody even bothered chasing.

After a twenty-ball lull in which England tried wearying him with a fifth-stump line, Smith swung a short ball from Overton so precisely through square leg that umpire Chris Gaffaney had to step to one side. In the opposite direction, he took Woakes through point with a blur of hands and the sharp jab of a horizontal bat. There is no name for this stroke, which is neither drive, cut, nor slash — its ancestry can only be a slice shot down the line.

A day that dawned promisingly for Smith's counterpart ended rather less so, although it was the batting rather than the bowling that shortfell its possibilities, six wickets for 38 in fifty deliveries continuing the travails of its tail.

Dawid Malan and Jonny Bairstow negotiated the first five overs as though they meant business, scoring one run. They tackled the next eight overs as if intent on rapine, ransacking 50. Malan threw his hands at Cummins and scythed over point, then karate chopped a ball past gully. A cut for four from Marsh raised England's record partnership against Australia at the WACA — now in all likelihood to stand for all time. Bairstow went to a fourth Test hundred, full of busy strokes and simple virtues, expressed, as it were, in his bat, plain as a plank of pine.

After drinks, however, Malan fell carelessly to Lyon, aiming over mid-on, and Smith reverted successfully to bounce, pace and peril, on a pitch suited to them, with formations to match. At one stage Australia's captain had every fielder behind square save short leg, who caught the cowering Overton; at another he had four fielders on the fence, as a retreating Broad hoisted a bouncer to the base of the light tower. Some other venue-specific shots were played: Bairstow obtained a boundary by punching Hazlewood into the tarmac-like square and bouncing it over point's head. But the innings ended abruptly enough that England's tail can hardly expect a ball in their halves the rest of summer.

As Smith came to the crease in the afternoon, the match was again in the balance, with Australia needing to bat last here, with the surface now exhibiting a few inconsistencies. England reprieved both Khawaja and Shaun Marsh. But Smith gave no chance, and any he might have offered would probably have been missed from sheer surprise. The only plans on his mind at the moment are his own.

THE SON ALSO RISES

16 December 2017

'A selector's job is interesting,' wrote Sir Donald Bradman in *Farewell to Cricket*, 'sometimes exasperating, occasionally heartbreaking.' He did not allow for it to be satisfying. Australia's panel chaired by Trevor Hohns have had a summer where they might beg to differ.

Shaun Marsh, Tim Paine, Cameron Bancroft: their selections, mainly intuitive rather than evidence-based, have borne fruit. Yesterday came the drop of the fourth shoe, Mitchell Marsh substantiating the case for his recall with a hearty, hairy maiden Test hundred. Between times, there was another hard day's Smith, on a pitch at its best, with the Australian captain's highest Test score providing an object lesson in avarice for runs which England would do well to heed.

It's more than six years since Marsh took first steps in international cricket, clouting four sixes in a T20 cameo at the Wanderers. He has been notable since, ironically, for flashes of promise undermined by a seeming diffidence, surprising in a cricketer with the pedigree of a champion and the physique of an Australian rules footballer. He has had some fine moments in limited-overs cricket, including a hundred against India last year, but the longer the game, it has appeared, the more time to think, to theorise, to fret.

Another Mitchell, Johnson of that ilk, diagnosed the complaint as one he knew full well: 'He just wants to do the best he can and do the job for the team, but occasionally you can see that he feels he is letting the team down.' At his half-century and century yesterday, he first gestured expansively to teammates, wreathed in smiles on the balcony, and only then acknowledged the rest of the spectators.

Actually, these spectators have never needed convincing: Perth fans have always regarded Marsh indulgently, as the SSOS, second son of Swampy. It's the rest of the country that has looked on sceptically, regarding him as a three-quarters-rounder, a part-day cricketer. Marsh talked before the game of having needed to decouple from social media for the sake of his clarity and confidence — one's modern critics come from all directions. Mind you, he had done nothing on the first two days here to discourage these detractors, bowling nugatory overs at medium pace and shelling a straightforward slip chance.

Yet this was the innings of a batsman rather than an all-rounder, played with native understanding of the importance of the V at the WACA and a weight of effortless power. Marsh is not a touch player — more touch-and-go. His check drives have a percussive force that sends mid-offs and mid-ons scrambling. When he attacks outright, they might as well hardly be there. One straight drive from Woakes yesterday would have rolled to Riverside Drive had buildings not interposed. He pulled Overton and Broad for boundaries after tea as if disposing of throwdowns.

Smith, ahem … if we are hardly running short of things to write about him, the sentiments are growing familiar. He yesterday became only the second batsman to reach 1000 Test runs in four consecutive years, a delivery reliability of which Amazon would be proud. His average swelled to a new peak of nearly 63, having doubled since his first Test century.

There are variations within this reliability. His first century here was his quickest (138 balls) just two Tests after his slowest (261 balls); he needed slightly longer over its sequel (163 balls), and there were periods where he was subdued, usually by attention on a fifth stump line, deliveries to which Smith prudently abjured a stroke.

As to who would blink first, there was never any doubt. Smith was always waiting, as he often seems to pause expectantly after his preliminary back-and-across step, not so much a trigger movement as a methodical bolt cocking. Then he would pierce another gap with a whirl of hands, or just as happily hop into a French cricket pose to defend off the back foot. Smith is a hard batsman from whom to look away, for there is something happening even when he lets the ball go, whether it's his withdrawing the bat like a magician pulling a tablecloth away, or his back foot kicking out afterwards like a skateboarder's hind leg.

Fully a third of Smith's runs accumulated through the covers. By rights, Australia's captain should struggle to cover drive, so far is his right hand round the handle, so far must his bat come from his backswing directed at point. But there is a sense that the rules do not apply to him, that he could bat on one leg if he chose, and that his hands seem to operate almost independently of each other, just as the pianist Glenn Gould used to record his hands playing separately. At the final drinks break, a retinue of four attendants ministered to him as he reclined in a plastic chair — he might have been borne from the arena at the close on a palanquin.

Otherwise, little was learned today so much as confirmed, that when there is no sideways movement to speak of, the members of England's attack succeed one another like right-arm automata programmed to propel at a delectable 130kmh. At Townsville, the visitors spent a whole day obtaining a single wicket against a junior XI; they hardly seemed likely to improve on that strike rate with Smith in this mood.

Root cudgelled his brains. Overton defied his broken rib. The Englishmen fielded well, and Bairstow was unobtrusively sound. The Barmy Army cheered loyally. They lacked not spirit but inspiration. Nor was there much to reproach England's selectors for. The only player who might have made a difference was not a choice available to them.

PERTH TEST DAY 4

ON THE BRINK

16 December 2017

Cricket careers almost inevitably end sourly. Otherwise, perhaps, they would not end at all. Alastair Cook and Stuart Broad have been valiant cricketers for England. But in this Second Test the game has tapped them on the shoulder, as they have seen others tapped.

A little over two years ago, Alastair Cook was a captain enjoying the thanks of a grateful nation for the recapture of the Ashes, Stuart Broad his right-hand match winner. A pathos was lent the occasion at Trent Bridge provided by Michael Clarke who was foreshadowing the end of his international career in the act of turning the urn over. Cook paid him generous tribute; Broad reflected afterwards on the eerie deadness in Clarke's eyes as the Australian captain went on his way in the second innings: 'He wasn't angry, he wasn't upset. He just looked gone.'

'Gone' is a word beloved of commentators. It has a different resonance for cricketers, implying a loss of powers, a blunting of edge, and a vulnerability that opponents are quick to sense. It's like the proverbial blood in the water, or bullet with your name on it, and no respecter of reputations.

Cook is thirty-two, Broad thirty-one — they are young men by any measure other than sport, where they are veterans, the former England's tallest Test scorer, the latter their second-highest wicket taker.

The Perth Test is Cook's 150th and the tenth anniversary of Broad's international debut. That sounds daunting enough, yet the truer measure is the sheer mileage on their cricket clocks: between them they have bowled and faced in the region of 30,000 deliveries, in the classical roles of opening batsman and opening bowler respectively.

That has been their glory; it has also, always, been freighted with risk. These are perhaps cricket's least forgiving roles, exposed by the merest loss of reflex for the batsman, the slightest loss of speed for the bowler, and once exposed there is little covering over. Fans hold them to exalted standards. Opponents know their methods. If not stationary targets, they are assuredly slower moving.

So it has been here. In the first innings, Cook was beaten by a fast, full delivery from Mitchell Starc that one suspected, not so long ago, he would have clipped comfortably through the leg side. Now it thudded into the pad on a contorted front leg, and he became just about the last batsman in this

Test not to review their dismissal, leaving with a sigh instead.

His second innings dismissal was perhaps still more worrying. What looked to the naked eye like a leading edge actually emanating from the middle of a crooked bat as it speared back to Josh Hazlewood who could hardly believe his good fortune. Neither attacking nor defending, neither committed nor withdrawing: it was a shadow shot for a darkening career.

Broad, meanwhile, returned figures of the kind that R. C. Robertson-Glasgow once called 'much ado about nothing': none for 142 from 35 overs. Again what was worse was his strange lack of presence. Tall, strong, fair-headed, never entirely without advice or histrionics, he has always stood out in a crowded attack. Here he shrank back to anonymity, much as he now does with the bat, with that exaggerated crouch and premeditated cower.

Gone tomorrow for certain will be the WACA, although it has signed off as a big cricket venue in a happier fashion. Its surface has been reintroduced as a character in its own right, an active agent in the direction of this match, offering something for everyone, except perhaps the 130kmh right-arm seam bowler — a type with which England, unfortunately, is overendowed.

The pitch presented yesterday morning with a scribble of cracks; whether it was imagination they seemed darker by afternoon. Tim Paine took guard well ahead of his ground in order to take them out of play — rather less of an option for Englishmen facing bowlers capable of velocities of 150kmh.

The sight of a ball from Broad jagging four degrees past Paine's edge, and a ball from Woakes running beneath Cummins' bat to arrive at Bairstow on the third bounce were perversely encouraging to the Australians. Mitchell Starc's extraordinary round-arm trimmer to bowl James Vince vindicated its promise.

On Friday night, members of the touring media were hosted at the state-of-the-art, $2 billion Optus Stadium which will host Perth's next international fixture come January, and an impressive sight it is too, with its lofty tiers, crewcut turf and sound and light show, suitably deafening and dazzling.

Football will embrace it; that it could hardly represent a greater change in local cricket culture has been reinforced these last four days, the WACA having been seen to picturesque advantage, bathed in warm but not hot sun, fanned by stiff breezes, occupied by happy spectators. The grassed areas were healthily populated, having arguably played their part in the WACA's eclipse by reducing its capacity in the early 1990s. That is the way of it, of course, but what Perth may gain in amenity it stands to lose in identity.

England, meanwhile, face rebuilding, as they did in 2013-14, when Cook brought to Australia an England team loitering palely. By its conclusion, Graeme Swann, Matt Prior and Kevin Pietersen had all played their last Tests, Pietersen involuntarily but irrevocably. What is prolonging the careers of Cook and Broad is now its own source of concern for England: the lack of recognizable alternatives.

PERTH TEST DAY 5

THE SHORT, SHARP SHOCK OF THE ASHES

17 December 2017

Cricket is getting shorter, and not just in the ways intended. It has taken Australia fourteen days to regain the Ashes that they lost in fourteen days just over two years ago. 'Dead Tests' may not be an inappropriate designation in the context of a trophy with funerary associations. But it sits oddly with 'live sport'.

Kudos to the Australians. They have played substantially the better cricket for significantly longer phases, and again yesterday, with Mitchell Starc, Patrick Cummins and especially Josh Hazlewood in full maraud. The two teams have not bowled on different pitches during this Test, but it has seemed like it.

Steve Smith, of course, has made run-making look almost recreational, his trademark the jogged leg-side single, registering in the steadily swelling score. The pitches on which he has batted this summer must have grown as familiar as his own garden.

England, meanwhile, have been locked ever tighter into a cycle of the bowling having to make up for batting having to make up for the bowling … with quite a lot of it to make up for absence of Ben Stokes. The crowd has grown used to it, too, not even troubling yesterday to boo Stuart Broad.

But 3-0 so soon? It leaves the summer's two showpiece Tests, Boxing Day in Melbourne and New Year's in Sydney with no bearing on the series. People will turn up. They loyally do. And it's hard to see Australia playing such demob happy cricket as England did at the Oval in 2015 when nothing was on the line. Yet if attention turned naturally to the Big Bash League, which commences tonight with its Sydney derby, it would be no wonder. Ebb and flow? More like crash through or crash.

Some of the reason was on show in the damp morning of the Third Test at the WACA Ground yesterday. There were mackerel skies, gloomy forecasts, flurries of inactivity. But the loss of overs was not, in the end, substantial. To be saved by weather today requires quantities of rain that call forth arks. Otherwise overs unbowled one day are added to subsequent days by reference to sliding scales that result in starting times of improbable precision, like 9.51am or 10.13am, but better value to spectators.

That leaves a lot of cricket to be played, and that it's as though the game has come to burn almost too brightly for sustainability. Since the glory days of 2005, there has been but one genuinely close Ashes Test, Trent Bridge in 2013. Otherwise the margins have been blow-outs, both ways. After only one series whitewash in the first 130 years of Anglo-Australia competition, there have been two in the last eleven years, and one would not bet against us watching the third. Certainly, a key indicator in this series has been the form of the captains, Smith and Joe Root averaging 142 and 29 respectively. If it cannot faithfully reflect their respective talents, it does index the degree to which Australia has overwhelmed its oldest rival.

Only once in the last fifteen years, moreover, has an away team won, as tours have grown more crowded, less forgiving. The 25 scheduled Test days of 2017-18 span 46 days in toto. Before them three low-key games in empty grounds; between them another. Little chance to prepare; no chance to recover. A five-Test series in these circumstances is squeezing a quart into a pint pot. Home ground advantage needs no further skewing.

That is not an excuse for England, any more than it was an excuse for Australia in 2015. Teams should not concede scores of nine for 622, any more than they should be bowled out for 60. But we are in an age of cricket and cricketers both impactful and brittle. Much attention, for example, has focused on Mitchell Starc's delivery to bowl James Vince on the fourth evening, deemed unplayable by many good judges. Yet it was surely significant how Vince chose to play Starc, bowling with a low-arm from round the wicket — naively showing all three stumps and attempting an attacking flick. Perhaps it was the difference between Vince's missing the ball by an inch and two feet. But, with his team three wickets down and 159 runs in arrears, it had a kamikaze quality. Root himself had already given way to his baser instincts, chasing a wide loosener from Lyon that he could only ever have nicked.

The Australians pursued their day fourteen goal with a studied relentlessness, undistracted by the inauspicious opening when the removal of the covers revealed hessian wet and surface moist from copious overnight rain, the effect worsened by the kind of intermittent sprinklings that leave you unsure whether to cancel your family barbecue. A slick ground staff can make the folding and unfolding of covers look like a routine at an Olympic opening ceremony. The hapless crew here resembled crewmen in a yacht race trying to secure a vagrant spinnaker. Reports came from the middle that the pitch was like, variously, playdough, plasticine, peat, treacle tart. There was time to muse on the collective noun for leaf blowers. A scattering?

An autumn?

When the sight of a white clad Smith jogging from the field at 12.50pm alerted onlookers to the imminence of play, it seemed likely to be brief, the cracks not quite as wide as in the WACA's glory days, but still a factor in the bowlers' favour and on the batsman's mind. Having bowled Bairstow beneath his bat, Hazlewood beat Moeen with a ball that did not so much deviate as detour.

In fact, the pitch cut few capers thereafter, and Hazlewood, the least of Australia's attack in Brisbane but the best here, bowled finely. And not an hour after the fall of the last wicket, it was raining again. England would wish it now to rain for the next month.

JOE ROOT AND STEVE SMITH
CAPTAINS ON A SEE-SAW
18 December 2017

English and Australian cricket teams travelling eastward from Perth yesterday were spread across a number of flights, although it so happened that the captains found themselves in the same business class section, separated by an aisle and a row. Joe Root sat by a window cradling his infant son, Steve Smith was plugged into his phone, both in their respective leisurewears. So much in common; such, at the moment, different trajectories.

Smith has the Ashes in his hands; Root has ashes in the mouth. Smith's team is the toast of his land; Root's is toast. Nobody is calling for Root's scalp, for his team's task was always an uphill one. All the same, he seems on an opposite roll. 'Winning is a habit, I believe,' he observed in his published account of the 2015 Ashes series, in which he was player of the series. 'Unfortunately, so is losing.' The Ashes of 2017-18 are proving that sentiment ever truer.

Ahead of time the Ashes were popularly framed as the head-to-head of two prentice captains — probably the first of a few. Just as Alastair Cook and Michael Clarke had three duels, it was possible to foresee 26-year-old Root duking it out with 28-year-old Steve Smith for some time to come.

In fact, it has been a catchweight contest, individually as well as collectively. Smith's average punch (142) has helped take three consecutive rounds off England; Root's (29) has bounced off a thick Australian hide. Root has now lost all seven of his Tests Down Under and is yet to make a hundred here — that's a tendency turning into a habit right there.

Root's first tour here four years ago was really the first setback to what had been a gilded career. He arrived as Cook's opening partner, having done the job in the northern summer, then at the last minute was demoted to number six. In the First Test, he recalled in his book, he was uprooted by Mitchell Johnson and whirled around by the gusts of Gabba hostility: 'It was almost too much for me, if I'm being honest.'

It was only the beginning. Root was not alone in being unsettled by the Australians' verbal incontinence: 'When Australia are on top they can get to you. One of their strengths is that they get tight as a team, become very vocal and aren't particularly nice with what they say.' But he was the one who began looking least himself. In the corresponding Test in Perth four years ago, he was sawn off in the first innings, guilty of an ill-advised review in the second. By the Sydney Test, he was an onlooker.

It's popularly imagined that such experiences toughen a cricketer, provide a motivation, stiffen his backbone and/or upper lip. Yet it remains unclear whether such cricket suits Root. One of his appeals has always been that he plays with a smile. When he cannot, a little something leaves his performance, and his inspiriting example. He has found himself on this tour dealing with events that would cloud any captain's face, and greeted them with growing world-weariness. The boyish Root, the reputed dressing room prankster, the cheeky chappy and sock snipper, has been nowhere to be seen.

Also absent from the dressing room, of course, has been Ben Stokes, who slotted in as vice-captain when Root succeeded Cook earlier this year, and who is a talismanic personality and cricketer round which others rally. Root retains strong and familiar support: assistant coach Paul Farbrace, for example, was his coach in the Yorkshire second XI. But Root has found himself taking up the morale slack. Michael Vaughan, a close confidante, said that as England captain sans Stokes this summer Root would have to 'lie a bit' about his team's chances. He has tried: after Brisbane, he insisted that England had outplayed Australia 'the majority of the time' on the first three days; after Adelaide, he described England as 'massively in the series'; after Perth, he said the margin was 'not a fair reflection' of how England have played and their 'really good performances'. But this last was an application for the vacancy left by Chemical Ali.

The chief disappointment has been Root's batting. He scoffed last month when Nathan Lyon said that the Australians were 'targeting' him. Yet Australians have been expert at potting visiting captains. Cook, MS Dhoni, Brendon McCullum, Misbah ul-Haq, Mahela Jayawardene, Jason Holder — none of these recent visitors have left this country with reputations enhanced. Perceptions have been accentuated by his rival. Smith has adapted to pace, bounce and conditions — his slowest Test hundred in Brisbane, his quickest in Perth. Root has become caught up in scoreboard scenarios, batting in each case under the cosh, coming in at 127, 17, 31, 54, 89 and 29 respectively. In 2015, he took advantage of the Australians' attacking lengths and fields, striking at 67 per hundreds balls; here he has been cut back to 53. In Brisbane the bowlers probed away at off and middle and trapped him on the crease; in Adelaide, they dragged him wide, aware that his instinct would be to assert himself; in Perth, again in search of runs, he succumbed to leg- and off-side strangles.

This will hurt Root's professional pride. He began the tour bracketed with batting's big beasts: not just Smith but Kohli and Williamson. He is falling away from that company in important measures, notably his conversion rate of thirteen hundreds from forty-seven fifties, and his distribution of scores, with only one second-innings hundred. When performance pales as games go deeper, questions of fitness and concentration arise. His mortal stroke on Sunday afternoon reeked of fatigue bordering on ennui. Quibbling with his captaincy has so far taken a low-key: it is the depth in his ranks and that state of England's game that make for richer talking points. But if England should incur defeat in Melbourne and Sydney, they must hope he is a Cook, who bounced back from his team's 0-5 defeat, rather than a Flintoff, who did not. England's captaincy can wear you out quickly. As Root disembarked in Melbourne, he was still wearing his sponsors' cap and hoodie. This is a job where you're never off duty.

BODY LANGUAGE
MANNERISMS MAKETH MAN
20 December 2017

Few batsmen in history have had such an idiosyncratic technique as
Steve Smith, with his backlift more of a sidelift, his trigger movements
as elaborate as loading a bolt action rifle. Fewer still can have had such a
repertoire of habitual gestures: the tactile preliminary inventory of his pads,
gloves, helmet and trousers, bat held upright; the stiff-legged double tap; the
bent-knee double dip; after each stroke, the signature followings through,
including, when he leaves the ball, a gesture of the bat as if bestowing a
knighthood, and a movement of the right arm as though slipping it into a
sleeve.

Far from random, it has a touch of the robotic; Smith admits to being
fussy and controlling, obsessed with his gear, averse to anyone touching
his bat during breaks in play out of superstition, insistent on taping his
laces tight to his shoes for neatness's sake. But it also follows in traditions
well-worn. A game of repetition and repose, cricket offers ample scope for
different methods and manners, quirks and quiddities.

Who has not picked up a bat and flourished it in the imagined manner
of a personal favourite? Who has not fancied themselves in a mould
of champion bowler or fielder? It is an expression of wonderment and
allegiance to mimic Dhoni's helicopter shot and Pietersen's switch hit, as it
was to emulate Ranji's glance and Hammond's cover drive. It might, though,
simply be about the way a player stands, moves, occupies space that detains
us. There is a T-shirt of a batsman's broad back, standing at the non-striker's
end, leaning on his bat with legs crossed. Although the face is obscure, you
know at once that the jaws would have been chewing his gum implacably,
because it is unmistakable as Viv Richards.

The custom of observation and emulation starts in childhood, where the
discovery of sport intersects with the world of make-believe. In *The Return
of the Ashes*, Mike Brearley describes the 3-year-old son of friends who
by shaping left-handed, tugging a cap low and swinging vigorously to leg
made himself into a facsimile of Australia's wicketkeeper Rod Marsh, with a
commentary to match: 'I'm Rommarsh. Square-cut.' Sometimes the homage
leads on to greater things. It was Viv Richards' lounging prowl and Sunil
Gavaskar's studious control that the boy Sachin Tendulkar used to imitate
in his colony games of tennis-ball cricket; it was Ian Chappell, with that

upturned collar, and Dennis Lillee, with his spreadeagling appeal, whom Shane Warne favoured in backyard Test matches against his brother. They matured into players with their own repertory of tics, notably Tendulkar's preparatory helmet tug and bow-legged squat, and Warne's languid hand-to-hand roll of the ball and adjustment of the shoulder of his shirt. But mostly, of course, we go living in our own heads, wondering what it feels like as we grow familiar with what it looks like, noting the similarities and differences, continuities and originalities.

In *How to Watch Cricket*, John Arlott urged that cricket's 'immense imaginative quality' was rooted in the habits of youth, never quite outgrown, of discerning character in distinction. 'Hero-worship is expected to disappear with maturity, and at its most idolatrous it is not a good thing for a man,' he said. 'But in watching a cricket match only a sheer dullard will fail to realize that he is not watching eleven identical and drilled dummies. All men are different, and their differences show on the cricket field. Cricketer after cricketer reveals his essential nature at this game.' Or so it seems — even if this is tantamount to the same thing.

It was, perhaps, ever thus. John Nyren's *The Cricketers of My Time* rejoices in the peculiarities of its characters. Billy Beldham had 'a peculiar habit of bringing his hand from behind his back immediately previous to his delivering the ball'; the Duke Dorset had 'a peculiar habit, when unemployed, of standing with his head on one side.' 'Short in stature' and 'swarthy as a gypsy', Noah Mann 'always played without his hat'; David Harris prepared to bowl by 'standing erect like a soldier at drill'; Lumpy Stevens celebrated wickets with a 'little grin of triumph'. These are cameos that vault cultures: C. L. R. James recalled reading them as a boy in Port-of-Spain and how he 'began to tingle'.

While there is a relative scarcity of directly descriptive writing about W. G. Grace and next to no footage, one idiosyncrasy is mentioned almost invariably: how he cocked his front toe when facing the bowler. As Sir Arthur Conan Doyle noted, Grace would 'slowly raise himself up to his height and draw back the blade of his bat while his left toe would go upwards until only the heel of the foot remained upon the ground'; it conveyed a cocky readiness, an imperious disdain. It was then, perhaps, the Edwardian embrace of style that put a premium on appearance and deportment. Victor Trumper was known by the neatness with which he folded his sleeves beyond the elbows — you can see it in George Beldam's sublime photograph of him. Generations of Sydney grade cricketers did the same, including Alan Kippax, who in his boyhood followed Trumper to every local game, with a scorebook in which he recorded only his hero's runs.

Jack Hobbs's custom of spinning the bat in his hands before facing up was immortalised in a cartoon by Arthur Mailey. Cecil Parkin's trick of flicking the fall from boot to hand was regarded as so novel as to feature in its own Pathe newsreel (https://www.youtube.com/watch?v=-q_J3F-qIH8), helping cement his reputation as cricket's great jester. As the distinctive grows familiar, in fact, the familiar turns suggestive. Philip Mead's range of cap tugs, bat pats, wiggles and shuffles suggested to R. C. Robertson-Glasgow 'the air of a guest who, having been offered a weekend by his host, obstinately decides to reside for six months.' Walter Hammond's walk to the wicket was in J. M. Kilburn's opinion 'the most handsome in all cricket', a flow 'linking stillness to stillness', inherently regal: 'He came like a king and he looked like a king in his coming.' Recalling the blue handkerchief that protruded from Lala Amarnath's trouser pocket, Vijay Hazare thought he displayed 'showmanship that would have been the envy of an advertising expert.' Citing Richie Benaud's plunging neckline and unrestrained appealing, Ray Robinson referred to Australia's great captain and guru as 'the spectator's best friend'.

After World War II, television and the age of mass reproduction brought appearance into sharper focus. The brylcreemed locks of Keith Miller and Denis Compton in the 1940s savoured of masculinity and sophistication; the probity of the 1950s, wrote Simon Rae, was somehow guaranteed by [Peter] May's immaculate parting'; the swing of the 1960s was caught in Ted Dexter's seigneurial bearing and the glint of the gold chain round Wes Hall's neck. By the 1970s, there were cricketers with a repertory of moves that would not have been out of place on the dance floor. Dennis Lillee choreographed his walk back so superbly that he needed only a casually outstretched right hand to accept the ball back, and a single right forefinger to flick the sweat from his brow.

Long careers leave deep traces on memory. Graham Gooch took guard proprietorially by displaying the full bat face in front of middle and leg; David Gower took his leave with a nonchalant tuck of the bat beneath his arm as though that was enough elegance for the day; Derek Randall jerked and twitched as though on a puppeteer's strings. A generation of Indians imitated Mohammed Azharuddin's upturned collars. Sri Lankans were intrigued by Sanath Jayasuriya's preparatory check off of all his gear. In the last couple of years of club cricket, I have seen batsmen fiddling with the Velcro on their gloves every bit as pedantically as MS Dhoni, and setting fields from the batsman's crease in the mode of Michael Clarke. In the case of 18-year-old Austin Waugh, the likeness is more than skin deep; he is the spit of his father Steve, in motion and at rest.

The gesture can also convey the autobiographical. It might tell us something of a cricketer's upbringing: Morne Morkel undertakes his anti-clockwise twirl at the end of his run because there was a lack of room in his local nets when he was growing up. It might relate something of their technical contemplations: Shane Watson's nervous adjustment of his back pad before every ball is a little *memento mori* of lbw. It might tell us something of a cricketer's belief system: Lasith Malinga applies a kiss to the ball before bowling because as 'a good Buddhist' fortunate enough to lead a comfortable existence he feels obligated to 'worship the ball that was what helped me get here'. In a recent interview concerning that fashionable notion of 'batting with intent', David Warner proposed a wide definition: 'Intent can be leaving the ball and your mannerisms around the crease. Those things bring a spark to my eye when I am at the other end. You know when your partner is on as well.' Warner's little limbo after taking guard, his loosening of the shoulders before he takes strike and of the wrist bands on his gloves when he is off-strike are fundamental to his ringcraft.

Warner's captain now intuits that he is being watched too. When Smith played and missed during his century in the Pune Test in February 2017, Ravi Jadeja cheerfully imitated his head toss, eliciting from Smith a smile of recognition. When Smith was beaten by a ball that kept low in Bangalore, Ishant Sharma responded with a range of grimaces, which the batsmen met with an insouciant head wobble, and the next ball an almost self-parodic leave. All part of the plan, he has said: 'I like to try and annoy them a little bit with some of my mannerisms rather than anything I say.'

Yet there remains a pleasing sense at such moments that we are seeing the player unguarded, themselves, whether it's Joe Root's warning against running by holding his bat vertically in his left hand like a stop sign, Stuart Broad's trio of jumps and scratches before bowling his first ball or James Anderson's adjustment of his forelock after each delivery. For all his vast experience, Alastair Cook still embarks on a run with an ungainly stride, as though he is a schoolboy slightly surprised to have made a good hit. Every so often, he will cup his glove to the side of his helmet to keep the world at bay, crouch and peer down the pitch to reorient in his surroundings.

To enjoy these little glimmers of imagined personality is also to express our freedom as spectators. Cricket is increasingly obsessed with action and spectacle, as though any pause for reflection or digression is against the spirit of entertainment — where television was once about conveying the live experience, the role of the live match now is to be more like television, a narrated whirl replete with replays and advertisements. To watch a player be themselves is to appreciate cricket's compounding of human material, its space and its scope. During his 239 at the WACA Ground, Smith faced 399 balls over twenty minutes short of ten hours while 505 runs were added. That's a lot of pads touches, bat taps and knee bends, but they all in their ways played a part.

WARNER IN EXCELSIS
26 December 2017

As drinks were served yesterday afternoon at the Melbourne Cricket Ground, the scoreboard stat-o-matic produced a figure for the crowd to chew on concerning the 'fastest Australian to 6000 Test runs'. There was Bradman, of course, in his role of everyday outlier; fourth in the list, slightly in arrears of Ponting and Hayden, came man of the moment David Warner, who had also just come by his twenty-first Test century.

The stat itself, of course, was something of a misnomer: the record, more precisely, concerned the fewest Test innings to achieve the relevant landmark, in this case 129. Yet how else does Warner come by records other than 'fast'? Since earning a T20 cap for Australia on this ground nearly eight years ago before playing a Sheffield Shield match for his state, his whole career has been headlong. Others may go further; Warner, as yesterday, takes an inside lane.

Before the match, Warner had spoken of wanting to defy the fields and lines that have kept him in slight check this summer, about 'staying out there and grinding it out and batting my way'. There was a touch of urgency when, playing with hard, tense hands, he looped his fifth ball just beyond gully's left hand, causing arms to be raised around the field.

Those English arms sank back and stayed there. Pretty soon, Warner was punching Broad and Anderson down the ground, pulling Woakes and Moeen, sweepers and the span of the ground constraining him square of the wicket, but little to be done in the compass's other degrees.

Mid-off, though set deep, seldom stood a chance when Warner leaned into his drives; he glanced Anderson with exquisite fineness. When others might have grown circumspect in the first session's last over from Moeen, Warner nonchalantly drove into the sightscreen on the full to reach 83. Bancroft went to lunch on a rather listless 19, like a rowboat that had been towed by a speedboat.

When a rock journalist once commented that the Ramones played short songs, Joey Ramone corrected him: they played ordinary songs really fast. So does Warner approach batting. It isn't impatience or impetuosity. It is his natural speed, almost a physical imperative, like a longer stride or a wider reach.

It's decelerating that feels more of a strain, as if the Ramones were essaying prog rock or a power ballad. Actually, his defence, straight and sculpted, is as solid as anyone's. But it's forcing bowlers and captains on the defensive that is his metier.

In this, of course, Warner is in step with a twenty-first century movement. As fast bowling has grown ever scarcer, fast batting, the kind heralded by the like of Virender Sehwag, and richly rewarded by T20, has come into its own. It was Sehwag who, when they played together at the Delhi Daredevils at the start of the decade, convinced Warner he had the method and mettle to adapt to cricket's longer forms, and seldom can counsel have been heeded with such alacrity; to this day, only Sehwag among specialist batsmen has a slicker Test strike rate.

At his pre-match media conference, interestingly, it was the example of Sehwag that Warner invoked, mentioning the measures that teams had taken to counteract his old Indian familiar: 'They had third man, two square legs and a deep point. They kept on bowling to his areas and strengths and he ended up getting out a couple of times but he worked it out himself. It's upon me to keep backing my strengths and playing my game.' Again with the 'my': it's as though Warner feels, perhaps since Sehwag's retirement, that the trademark, at least in Test cricket, resides with him.

Whatever the case, yesterday was batting as thinking aloud: a half-century in 64 balls, a century in 66 more, restrained only as the milestone approached, by some cagey denial. Joe Root, doggedly, packed the off side. Stuart Broad, patriotically, bowled wider still and wider. At last, on 99, Warner was guilty of trespass. Trying to force the issue against Tom Curran, he miscued to Broad at mid-on, marching smartly for the pavilion, then turning just as smartly back when the replay screen revealed a transgression of the front line. Warner being Warner, he could not refrain from needlessly rubbing this in, gloating in the good fortune that had deprived Curran of a maiden Test cricket — a puerile and unnecessary demonstration.

As it happens, nicking off to a handy delivery from Broad a few overs later, Warner did not linger. Others rather did, on a pitch that does not bode well from either a result or Test cricket. To tea, the three other Australian batsmen on show during the day had struck at 24 per hundred balls, cricket's version of a two-speed economy. Resuming afterward, Steve Smith provided the stimulus for a broader-based growth.

Australia's captain is as sure as his vice-captain is fast, comfortably banking a half-century in 98 deliveries, sometimes, when Curran bowled another of his rather too-frequent slower balls, appearing almost to have slowed down time. Smith had come into the match with an injured bottom hand; he could probably have batted with it tied behind his back.

After Warner's helter-skelter, Root could feel as though he had escaped damage too severe. His counterpart, however, has not been dismissed in a Test match at the MCG since 28 December 2014, in which time he has come by 434 runs. The scoreboard might need to have statistics readily to hand today.

MELBOURNE TEST DAY 2

COOK'S TOUR

27 December 2017

Cricket is often called an individual game in a team setting. If this definition is allowed, the term 'dead' Test will ever be a misnomer. There will always be personal points to prove, singular purposes to be pursued. It even makes a certain sense in this context that England, relieved of the Ashes, have an edge in this Fourth Test: their individuals have by far the most ground to make up.

It was hard to choose who had the poorer WACA Test out of Alastair Cook and Stuart Broad. The pitch seemed simultaneously too fast for Cook, too slow for Broad, the Australians too much for either, and the Ashes too hot to hold.

They are cricketers of a certain age, with great records, and maybe also dwindling motivations. No Englishman has scored more Test runs than Cook; only one has more wickets than Broad. Where else to go? What else to prove? There was even a school of thought that England might do without them in Melbourne, although it was far from obvious who would take their places. They had toiled in the nets before the game like ascetics. 'Dead' Test? Not here; not now; not for either man.

If Cook's 150th Test had looked perilously like a cricket funeral, his 151st has now unfolded into a disarmingly cheerful wake. His thirty-second Test century was no dogged entrenchment. From the first it was positive, even in defence, his body forming strong shapes, his bat erecting broad barriers.

For a batsman otherwise so prudent, too, Cook rather revels in the hook and pull, which he's prepared to play in the air — sometimes, as in Brisbane, to his cost. Yesterday, he was determined to get it right. First he almost dragged Jackson Bird on; next he miscued Josh Hazlewood; at last, as Pat Cummins dropped short, he nailed it, and flourishingly — had the shot peeled from Kevin Pietersen's bat it would have been called flamboyant.

Cook followed up with a cover drive off the front foot — a shot he essays with such contrasting rarity that it often seems like a harbinger, cricket's equivalent of spring's first swallow. It was not seen again, but after further boundaries down the ground and through gully, Steve Smith posted a deep backward point, two-thirds of the way to the rope. Still more surprisingly, Cook picked the man out thrice, for long singles. Good captaincy, but also a tiny concession — Australia's captain, with the Ashes in his pocket, was defending, against Cook, as his formidable pacemen bowled.

Luck came Cook's way, as it must: Smith shelled an edge at slip, perhaps unsighted by Paine, who had just gone up to the stumps. As the day ended, Smith then sought to pray on a memory, having ended a long Cook vigil with minutes of a day to go during the 2015 Oval Test. This time, however, he provided an over of amiable dross enabling Cook to add another record to his bulging hoard — a century at each Australian Test venue on which he has played.

Actually, the Australian attack for the first time this summer seemed stretched. Mitchell Starc was unavoidably missed. From lengths where the ball had flown in Perth, nicks were here barely carrying to slip. Though he executed another of his India rubber man return catches, Lyon obtained more turn when he heaved a beach ball back into the crowd.

Hazlewood plugged away nobly, but Bird and Mitchell Marsh could find little assistance, while Cummins was reportedly stricken with stomach trouble. His second ball after tea was a 133km/h half-tracker which Cook yanked through mid-wicket as though knocking off a flower with a walking stick. When Cook punched the last ball of the same over through the off-side, Cummins seized his sun hat and glasses dreaming of a palm tree at fine leg to lie under.

It was not as the day had begun, even before it began, as it were. The overnight Australian batsmen materialised by their gate at 10.22am, fully eight minutes before the scheduled resumption, as though they could not wait to be amongst it, on a day forecast to reach 35 degrees. Shaun Marsh already had his lid screwed on; Smith was performing flexes and squats, having not been dismissed in an MCG Test since it was 1924 on *Downton Abbey*.

Yet there was a hint of avidity about the Australians at the crease after their advance by 2.7 run per over increments on the first day, as there had been during their second innings in Adelaide. Smith became the first of three batsmen to drag attacking shots onto their stumps. Marsh planted his front leg, and perished on review; Lyon played around his, requested a review, then promptly headed off. England's bowlers, who have looked at times during this series content with a situation of armed neutrality pursued directions more aggressive — and as Brian Statham once philosophised, where's the point of running in thirty yards to watch a batsman shoulder arms?

Experienced Broad watchers on the first day had reported more of the old pump of his knees and pull of his levers. It was complemented on the second with more presence, more of his old villainy. Early on, Broad picked up a ball in his follow-through, backhanded at the strikers' stumps and broke them, even if Smith and Marsh spoiled the *mot juste* by taking a run. Broad seethed, stalked back, and kept running in, appreciably faster on this far slower pitch than in Perth — a rough measure of effect, but not an unreliable one. He did not squander energy on bouncers, was prepared to be driven, and collected two lbws. His nine wickets this series have still cost 40 each. But by bridging the long gap between the fifth and sixth, he has established something to build on.

For Australia, of course, there is the opposite challenge to England's in this match. They have secured the prize after giving their all, which to draw on leaves only hidden reserves. There has not been an end-of-school feeling to their cricket these past two days, but maybe an end-of-term one, and becomingly so: they applauded Cook's milestone last night with gratifying generosity. Bear in mind that England had their best, or least bad, moments of the 2013-14 Ashes here in similar circumstances, a 0-3 deficit: they secured a first-innings lead before slumping by nine wickets. Yet the story of the Ashes itself contains the possibility, if not the promise, of rebirth, and it's been a pleasure to watch two fine players live again.

MELBOURNE TEST DAY 3

BIG DADDY

28 December 2017

Alastair Cook's original batting mentor Graham Gooch had a mild obsession with 'daddy hundreds' — the standard century being treated as a jumping off point for vaster accumulations. As a coach, he hammered it from a slogan into a cliché, a solution for every cricket ailment.

Like most clichés, it has an undeniable appeal, even an inherent logic. There should, on the face of it, be no better time to bat — no more contented state of mind in cricket — than with a hundred against one's name on a scoreboard. Cook came to his third day task at the MCG yesterday with the further boost of overnight rest and collegial approbation. Daddy hundred? He'd have been considering invitations for the uncles and aunts too ....

For all that, the daddy hundred is not so easily done — indeed, that is what makes it notable, a kind of feat in its own right. One must be fit. One must be dogged. One must be hungry. Steve Waugh turned fourteen of his thirty-two Test hundreds into 150s; Mark Waugh wrung only one from his twenty.

Test cricket does funny things to people. Yesterday it had Joe Root holing out with a game at his mercy. It occasioned such paralysis in Dawid Malan that he did not feel his leaving a splinter in the ball; it induced in Moeen Ali such frenzy that he seemed to be auditioning for the Big Bash League.

Test cricket, however, does not to funny things to Cook. He had marked his 33rd birthday the day before the match nursing a summer's average of 13. But his century celebration at the end of the second day had been typically understated, maybe even considered: no need to waste energy; no cause for triumphalism on a tour that has in most respects been a failure.

For all that, his average hundred coming to Melbourne was 155 — not perhaps as high as one would have expected for a batsman who has piled as many as 294. Accidents happen; best-laid plans go astray; even good Alastair nods off sometimes.

So to the third morning. Cook added 16 in the first hour, 14 in the next, biding his time, husbanding his powers. He is not at the crease a slow mover, yet is also somehow never hurried: he drops into his stance just before the bowler turns, both polite and ever-ready. He checks his guard every so often with a single dainty hand, re-enacts his defensive alignments with a gesture like someone looking intently at a painting to see if it is hanging quite straight. And when set, as yesterday, he just goes on piling up runs in quantities never gross or tasteless.

At times it was almost possible to forget Cook was there, to concentrate on something else, to drift off and drift back. He does not demand your attention or approval. During recent press conferences, David Warner has talked about having at times to subdue his desire to dominate bowlers and opponents, to 'take the ego out' of his batting. Cook must have an ego — no performer can command a stage without it. But one imagines him leaving it tucked tidily into the corner of his cricket bag before he heads out.

His strokes yesterday contrived to be both distinctive and unostentatious, his straight drive a cautious shove, his square cut a wispy slash. All day *Cricinfo*'s metrics were listing his most 'productive shot', responsible for more than a quarter of his runs, to be the 'flick', which presumably encompasses the pat, dab, nudge and nurdle.

Cook's grip is low and the face of his bat closed, a measure he adopted after an unsuccessful first Australian tour having studied the techniques of Australian opponents such as Matthew Hayden and Justin Langer who were hardly ever caught behind the wicket — even then he knew he'd be back, was thinking four years ahead.

That preparation paid off in 2010-11, availed him nought in 2013-14 when his team's performance was, as Cook confessed, 'the worst I had ever felt about anything.' In this sense, you could say that Cook was returning in this Test match to the scene of some of England's best and worst moments in his career. But that would be a banality, for it is true wherever Cook goes now: he is hardly doing anything in his career now for the first time. His achievement is that he continues to attack each day afresh, unencumbered, ungrudging, apparently unboreable by what at times must be a tortuous monotony.

Between lunch and tea yesterday, Cook accrued a further 39. Steve Smith was scratching his head for solutions, at stages forming as many as six fielders into an off-side crescent for an errant drive on a slightly two-paced pitch. Cook punched forward and cut back, with that compact stiff-armed swing, like one of the little figures in the table top Test Match game.

By tea, Cook had batted four sessions, and his innings had unobtrusively assumed daddy hundred dimensions; now came a Father's Day surge towards stumps, as England added 131 runs in 31 overs. Cook hit no better shot than a square drive off Hazlewood to go to 190, no more surprising shot than a lofted straight drive from Lyon to go to 195, no more satisfying shot than the straight drive that raised his double hundred. At last Cook had found a partner to stand by him, Stuart Broad, which itself strained credulity, for Broad throughout the tour has shown all the stickability of Teflon. Yet this is another quality of daddy hundreds: like a strong but benevolent patriarch, they coax the best from others.

MELBOURNE TEST DAY 4

KEEPING THE FAITH

29 December 2017

Not every contest in cricket is vivid and decisive; most, in fact, pass without our registering them. One just before lunch at the Melbourne Cricket Ground yesterday lasted only seven deliveries, while offering something like a crossroads on a crossroads.

For both Usman Khawaja and Moeen Ali, 2017-18 loomed as a crucial Ashes, in roles identifiably central, respectively first-wicket down and key all-rounder. Additionally, of course, they have their faith in common. But the cricket challenges they are facing are mirrors of one another, involving the gap between their performances at home and away.

For Khawaja, this series should have been something of tonic after a year more out than in due to a perceived inertia against slow bowling, including a tour of India as a supernumerary and a tour of Bangladesh as a casualty. In Australia the last couple of summers, he has caught the eye as much as anyone, with batting of exquisite touch rather than power, averaging twice what he does abroad. Homecoming, then, offered the opportunity for re-establishment.

For Moeen, the task was as tough as he has been set in his four years of international cricket. He has been a matchwinner with bat and ball on his own surfaces, but abroad has been chosen *faute de mieux*. In Australia he was bound to be challenged, as many a finger-spinner before him: the 21st century examples of Richard Dawson, Ashley Giles, Graeme Swann and Monty Panesar boded ill.

Both have disappointed these adjusted expectations. Khawaja has compiled two rather anonymous fifties, and averaged 28; with three expensive wickets and 136 runs in seven innings, Moeen has been a shadow of the all-rounder who followed an unbeaten 75 in 66 balls with a hat-trick in Manchester less than six months ago. Each has wandered the outfield as if involved in other games, or perhaps games within games, participating in the Ashes but not quite fully involved.

Their encounter yesterday was likewise glancing and insubstantial. Khawaja came to the crease just as Joe Root had offered Moeen some therapeutic overs in a period of relative calm. He patted back four deliveries, charged a fifth, lofting it beyond mid-off, where it was gleefully caught by a man in a lilac shirt; after another delivery, he drove easefully to the cover boundary.

Moeen gave way apologetically to Stuart Broad; Khawaja gave way promptly to Steve Smith by nicking off to James Anderson. So continued a tale of low-key woe, one cricketer beset by adversity, another unable to grasp an advantage.

Moeen's predicament on this tour has been aggravated more than most by the absence of Ben Stokes, whose gap in the batting order he was expected to fill in addition to his anticipated bowling burden. In England the last few years he has been a delicious luxury at numbers seven and eight, all exotic strokes and signature flourishes licensed by the company of the tail; at number six in Brisbane and Adelaide he seemed torn between reflex and responsibility.

Even in his old slot here, he has appeared unsure whether to stick or twist. His response of throwing caution then his wicket to the wind, falling for the sixth time to his counterpart Nathan Lyon, hardly befitted a player scheduled to play his fiftieth Test in New Zealand.

Moeen also came into the series restricted by injuries first to his side and then to his spinning finger. The impairment to his mechanics can only be guessed at; probably the greater blow was to his confidence, given Moeen's propensity for classifying himself a 'second spinner' even when there is no first.

The role of all-rounder can cut both ways. It offers prompt redemption: failure in one skill can be immediately counteracted by success at the other. It can also tighten a spiral, where lost faith proves infectious. That was the weight of Moeen's unsparing self-appraisal after the Adelaide Test: Moeen had, he felt, 'let down the team and the captain', and also that the tour had shown where he was 'as a cricketer and a spinner'.

If the suspicion of Moeen might be that he demands overmuch of himself, the opposite is speculated about Khawaja. Certainly he is becoming rather a whetstone for opinion. During this Test he has received the backing of Mike Hussey, who believes he should form part of Australia's starting XI in all forms of cricket at home and away, and the scolding of Ian Healy, who thinks he 'needs to get going and get his career kickstarted again' or he will 'get in a bigger hole'.

The views are not necessarily contradictory: indeed, both reflect a sense that Khawaja is in a rut, that neither he nor his team are obtaining the mileage from his talent they should. It will not improve his away record if he is not picked; nor does it help his case that he remains an indifferent fielder, and runs between wickets like Bartolo Colón runs bases.

Here are two capable cricketers, then, at sensitive junctures, where their next steps will be important to how their careers are evaluated. Perhaps they will find solutions; but perhaps, too, they will not, and have, without us knowing, reached the limits of their potential.

Khawaja is 31, Moeen in his 31st year. Cricket is demanding, never more various or athletic, closely analysed, critically examined. Modern professionalism, coaching and high-performance programmes seem to hold out a promise of perpetual incremental improvement and always expanding frontiers; common sense says this must be an illusion, that sooner or later every cricketer ceases to develop, maybe treads water, maybe sinks, and that there is in this really no disgrace. Not everyone will be great; for all manner of reasons, some will have to rest content with being exceedingly, exceedingly good.

TIME STANDS STILL

30 December 2017

An old adage holds that one should never judge a cricket pitch until after both teams have batted on it. On the surface prepared for the Fourth Test at the Melbourne Cricket Ground, a third team could have batted, and maybe a fourth, into 2018. It might have been showing wear by Australia Day, playing at variable heights by Easter. Multi-storey carparks have deteriorated more quickly.

Just as well, then, that Tests last only five days, for it spared the public more cricket like the concluding Saturday — an experience equivalent to repeated listening to an Andre Rieu Christmas album. Australia were meant to be playing England. In the end, both teams ended up competing with the conditions. The conditions won. Which made cricket the loser. 'Drop-in pitch' hardly does it justice. In the same sense, perhaps, is a corpse a 'drop-in human body' ….

Steve Smith made the best of things, steadily stalking his twenty-third Test century, eight of them in his last thirteen Tests. He had been guilty of a certain impatience in the first innings, helping a ball onto his stumps with a diagonal bat. Now he was unyielding as what he was batting on.

A murmur was heard when Warner holed out attempting a sweep, a shot as flawed in execution as selection that could really go in no direction but vertically. A tremor was felt when Shaun Marsh nicked off on the eve of the second new ball.

After lunch, Broad defeated Mitchell Marsh's outside edge twice, induced him to carve just short of backward point and appealed for a leg-side strangle. But the ball's capers soon abated, and Smith seemed as likely to get out as Stonehenge to fall over. By 5pm he and Marsh were walking off with the smiles of men who had discharged a tedious but necessary job, quietly satisfied.

One of the few other smiles must have been worn by Mitchell Starc, who had he brought his injured heel into this game would by now be preparing to have his gangrenous leg amputated. For the rest of us, it was a day we shall never get back, less reminiscent of Alastair Cook than Alistair Cooke when in one of his broadcasts he described cricket to Americans as a 'ceremonial coma'.

Players do bear a certain indirect responsibility for such tedium. Modern batsmen discombobulated by the slightest sideways movement encourage the preparation of pitches benign enough for games go the distance. But there's a reason Steve Harmison spoke of 'chief executive pitches'. They arise from the uniformity beloved of managerialism, that seeks to fashion commodity product for commodity audiences.

On the first day, Cricket Australia chief executive James Sutherland urged onlookers to suspend judgement, saying it was 'too early to judge' the pitch, and that they should 'see how everything unfolds on the park'. Except it didn't. In the first session of the second day, seven wickets fell; in fourteen further sessions, seventeen wickets. So now is the perfect time to judge, after the showpiece Test of summer was rendered farcical, and by the chief executives' own criteria.

In February 2017, the chief executives' committee of the International Cricket Council foreshadowed a system of demerit points for sub-standard pitches and outfields. It primarily had in mind the proverbial twenty-two yards of batting hell that ends Tests in three days or fewer; but it also mooted sanction for pitches offering 'little or no seam movement or turn at any stage in the match together with no significant bounce or carry, thereby depriving the bowlers of a fair contest between bat and ball'. Which sounds an awful lot like Josh Hazlewood's assessment of the MCG's qualities: 'It's quite evenly paced, there's no real sideways movement, no real swing and it doesn't spin much.' Apart from that a pretty good deck, eh Josh?

Luckily for the MCG, the system commences operation next year. Still, fifteen minutes after stumps were drawn, the Melbourne Cricket Club issued a mea minima culpa, promising to 'take on board feedback from the players, umpire and cricket bodies' about what it consented was a surface without 'the pace and bounce that we had expected'.

The club pointed out that the MCG has used drop-in pitches since 1996; what it didn't say was that on recent evidence they have deserved to dropping into the sea afterwards. Since England last played here, Australia have drawn a Test against India containing almost 1500 runs, won a Test against Pakistan who obligingly self-destructed in two sessions after four days of fifteen wickets for nearly 1000 runs, and won a Test against West Indies after declaring its first innings at three for 551.

The Test comes at a tipping point in Australian cricket: a wealthy sport that wrings its hands about Test cricket's challenges, while ignoring those of its own making. It is about to inaugurate a new international venue, Optus Stadium, with another drop-in pitch; it has just kissed off the WACA Ground, whose built-in pitch was the best of summer. Cricket spends a lot of time talking about innovation, but not much money. If drop-in pitches in multi-sport stadiums are the future, then maybe it's time to invest in improving the quality of their pitch preparation technology. At least the campaign for four-day Tests suffered a setback here. Unfortunately, so did the campaign for five-day Tests.

ALASTAIR COOK

BATTLING ON

31 December 2017

The tone was soft, the eyes downcast, the smile shy. The speaker scratched behind his ear, stroked his mandible. The sentiments were honest but not maudlin, mainly of relief, seasoned with some regret.

The Melbourne Test involved more than one vintage Alastair Cook performance. Not only was Cook on the field for the entirety of the game, but he put in extra duty at the press conferences, as double-centurion and man-of-the-match. Walking off at the end of day three, he first dealt politely with Mark Taylor on the boundary line — he looked astoundingly fresh, as though he could immediately have gone around again. Then he presented before the written press, many of whom had recently doubted his ability to come back after five Tests without a fifty. Cook had news: so had he.

Media conferences are a routine of the tour, a bugbear for players but seldom onerous, because they are usually appearing in the context of success. There's the opportunity for some schadenfreude, maybe a bit of braggadocio, of which several Australians have taken advantage this summer. Cook started instead by reflecting on his failures coming into the game. 'All tour I've been struggling with rhythm,' he confessed. 'I've actually been embarrassed about my performances.'

Had he felt his place in question? 'They would have been entitled to drop me, just because I literally hadn't scored a run since Edgbaston.' Had he doubted himself? 'One hundred per cent. I've doubted myself for twelve years. I'll probably continue to doubt myself. The longer it goes, the harder it becomes. That's why I'm quite proud, going to the well again and delivering a performance. It's just a shame it's four weeks too late [to help retain the Ashes]. I'll have to live with that for a long time.'

Funnily enough, psychologising Cook has been a popular hobby of this tour. Old rivals such as Ricky Ponting and Mitchell Johnson have doubted whether he retained the 'fire in his belly' to continue. Old teammates Kevin Pietersen and Graeme Swann have wondered 'how hungry he is to carry on'. Interestingly, Cook excluded this from his self-analysis: he ascribed his lack of form mainly to the faltering sync in his trigger movements. But perhaps it was audible in that homelier metaphor of 'the well', with its hint of a finite supply — an acknowledgement that he might return one day and find it empty.

Certainly it was the antithesis of a press conference another opening batsman held three weeks ago. Asked after the Bangladesh Premier League final whether his 146 not out off 69 balls entitled him to be considered the Bradman of T20, Chris Gayle responded: 'No, I am actually the greatest batsman of all time.' It was classic hashtag bait, fodder for a five-minute Twitter furore.

Cook neither plays T20 nor is on Twitter, and in his presence you could sort of see why, that it's a matter of attitude as well as aptitude. 'Most of my runs are pretty ugly runs,' he conceded. 'It's quite hard work.' Asked about surpassing Brian Lara's runpile, he shrugged his shoulders: 'I can't really explain that. I just feel sorry for Brian Lara.' This was not the feigned modesty of 'I'm-just-happy-to-contribute-it's-all-about-the-team', but an entirely genuine humility.

There must, of course, be a part of Cook that savours the battle, the sense of genuine measure, however cruel and unsparing. Short-form cricket not only accents the exhilarating and explosive, it relieves obvious responsibility. The batsman never need feel truly defeated: it was the game that made you do it. The bowler can cop it sweet: the reality is that sometimes you will go the journey. With Test cricket, as is often observed, the name is on the tin. And tests get failed, chasteningly, sometimes depressingly. I cannot tell whether a humbling game has made Cook a humble man, or whether as a humble man he suits a humbling game, but they do seem strangely bound together.

It may be Cook's limitation that he is confessedly susceptible to doubt, cannot simply shrug it off, feels the burden of failure, can only allow himself to feel 'quite proud' in success — some would identify it as a clear case of the English talent for morbid self-deprecation. But it also has an authenticity that's disarmingly relatable. When Cook reached his double century, every Australian clapped — and I mean seriously clapped. A few stopped after a while, others went on. Mitchell Marsh at cover kept applauding as the bowler walked all the way back. His face wore a broad smile. He has lately bounced back from a long period of enfeebling doubt, and anxiety about letting his teammates down, to taste his first real Test success. There was assuredly something in Cook's innings for every cricketer who has known how harsh the game can be and wondered if they could put themselves through it again.

At the close, Australian players came from every corner of the ground to shake Cook's hand, which was a fine tribute, for Cook does not play cricket in that rather self-praising, prolier-than-thou 'Australian way', of always 'moving the game on', of 'there is a line you can't cross'. But Australians also put store in fronting up, in stoicism and resilience, in toil and faith. It was a double century against Australians, for Essex at Chelmsford in 2005, that first presented Cook's credentials as a potential Test cricketer. And here he was more than a dozen years later still shaping up against them. That sort of endurance wins a lot of credit hereabouts. Cook has won the Ashes and defended them, been beaten and come back for more. The Fifth Test this week, his 152nd, will be his last in these parts. More than a few locals will wish him well.

JAMES ANDERSON

JIMMY'S FINAL LAP

January 3 2018

Australians have never warmed to James Anderson. The feeling may be mutual. In his autobiography, he recalls his first Test tour as uniquely unpleasant, in a social as well as a sporting sense: 'Australia is home to some of the most poisonous creatures on earth, and most of them seemed to dwell on the streets of Sydney and Melbourne.'

Some time in the next few days, 35-year-old Anderson will take his last new ball for England in an Australian Test match, probably with few regrets — he'll hardly be sought out for a testimonial by Kookaburra. Yet few cricketers of his time have been more stealthily remarkable.

So many records did Alastair Cook and Steve Smith leave in their respective wakes in Melbourne that another passed unnoticed. By playing his 133rd Test, Anderson became Test cricket's most capped pace bowler, overtaking Courtney Walsh. The only bowler to have played more Tests is Shane Warne; the rest of those ahead of Anderson on the list, Jacques Kallis and Mark Boucher apart, are specialist batsmen.

Anderson has endured in his uniqueness too. At 188cm, he stands only 5cm taller than his boyish captain Joe Root. At 76kg, he weighs about the same as his bantamweight antagonist David Warner. He should hardly bowl 100kmh, let alone 135kmh.

These Ashes are an advertisement for fast bowling as an occupation for giants: both attacks are composed of towering men, while Australia is breeding monsters like Billy Stanlake and Peter George. Anderson belongs to a more ancient lineage, of smaller figures, compact and rhythmic, like Ray Lindwall (178cm) and Harold Larwood (173cm), although he is more lightly built than either, while no cricket or conditioning coach would recommend the way he rotates his back and completes his action by looking at the ground.

Yet there is no evidence of his performances attenuating — on the contrary. Since turning 30, in an era of flat pitches, fat bats and machine-stitched balls, Anderson has taken 254 Test wickets at 24.15. In 2017 alone, he claimed 55 victims at 17: almost twice as many wickets at less than half the cost of his old confrere Stuart Broad, four years his junior. The skill he has polished to a remarkable lustre has been bowling at left-handers, and from over the wicket, departing the round-the-wicket angle that for a long time was a default mode among faster bowlers.

For a pace bowler, Anderson wastes nothing: his run is economical, his follow through abbreviated, his walk-back brisk; he gets through overs in almost one continuous motion, as though to leave the batsman, like Rosencrantz and Guildenstern, no shriving time. The problem for England this summer is that Anderson has not been able to bowl all the time, although he has done his best, delivering more overs (189.3) and giving up runs more grudgingly (2.2 an over) than anyone on either side. England had similar problems here four years ago. It is a damning comment on their cricket that while Australia has remade its attack almost entirely in the interim, English bowling still consists of Anderson, Broad, TBA, A. N. Other and Subject to the Crown Prosecution Service.

So why the reluctance to extend admiration? Anderson is partly penalised for his excellence at home. Using his own pitches, overhead conditions and cricket balls he has taken 335 wickets at 24.29; his record away is 187 wickets at 32.8, leading to his derogation as an 'English bully'. Yet Mitchell Johnson paid 25 for his wickets at home and 32 away, and nobody here considers him an 'Australian bully'. Nor, save in his career's earliest stages, has the gap between Anderson's best and worst ever been so pronounced as Johnson's.

There is also that Anderson is a notoriously ornery opponent — proud, perfectionist, prickly. It does not seem anything personal. Anyone in range with a bat becomes a target. The first time they were formally introduced as English players, having previously only been county opponents, Alastair Cook noted: 'The last time we met you called me a cunt.'

It's not obvious whether his verbals have ever actually intimidated anyone: Brad Haddin said he found that his opponent's northern accent rendered Anderson's sledging unintelligible. If anything they may have stimulated the competitive juices of others. In his autobiography, Chris Rogers noted that England's verbal hostility in the 2013 Ashes inculated a sense that 'these guys need to be put in their place' in 2013-14.

In Anderson's case, the on-field abrasiveness has in part been to compensate for an off-field reticence. Indeed, it has been cultivated with the help of psychologist Mark Bawden, so that the warrior persona 'Jimmy' is distinguishable from the shy homebody 'James', whose friends of longest standing are those he made at the outset of his career at Burnley CC, his 185-year-old Lancashire League club.

This means, I suspect, that Anderson has never quite been able to negotiate dealing with opponents as anything other than that. There's no deficiency in this — in some ways it is a form of sincerity, and it is an issue that each cricketer must solve must solve according to their own lights. But it has, I think, hindered appreciation of an unusually diverse and thoughtful athlete.

This summer Anderson is contributing to an engaging BBC Radio 5 Live podcast, 'Tailenders', with his friend Felix White, founder of the indie pop group the Maccabees. He's relaxed, dryly humorous, loyal to his team, and sometimes very insightful. Anderson's passion for music extends to his being a long-time supporter of a music therapy charity, Nordoff Robbins. He was also executive producer of an excellent documentary, *Warriors* (2015), about Kenya's soul-stirring Maasai Warriors cricket team.

I happened to attend this film's launch in London, and was struck by Anderson's presence. He was clearly conscious that his involvement had drawn a sizeable proportion of the audience, yet equally abashed about it, and anxious not to distract from the work of the film's director Barney Douglas. In such glimpses can be the measure of a man.

I wondered why the subject had appealed to Anderson. Perhaps it's that, in his own way, he is also a tribal man, loyal and wary. It will be interesting to see how one who has expressed so much of his personality through cricket comes to terms with life beyond it; in the meantime, take the opportunity these next five days to study one of the game's finest craftsmen.

SYDNEY TEST DAY I

THE ROOT OF THE PROBLEM

4 January 2018

Before this Fifth Test, Joe Root mused that the difference between the teams during these Ashes had been Steve Smith: 'Take his runs out of it and we've been there or thereabouts to win.'

More meaningless than obvious, or vice versa? Reminiscent certainly of that old gag about the anatomical difference between your aunt and uncle. The point might also have been more sharply made as the difference between Smith and Joe Root.

As vice-captains in 2015, the pair split nearly 1000 runs, compiling two centuries apiece, in winning causes each time. They stood for both present and future, storied careers of Ashes rivalry almost foreordained. Thirty months, however, have changed that rivalry's dynamic. In 2015 his team's victory made Root the obvious recipient of the Compton-Miller Medal for Player of the Series; this summer's medal has surely already been sent for engraving with his counterpart's name.

Coming into the Sydney Test, Smith had made more than twice the runs of Root at four times the average. The Australian's three hundreds, moreover, have been defining: the Englishman's three fifties have been arrested developments, which his career in a general sense, with a single century in his last eighteen innings, has started to look also.

What was left for Root yesterday could only be the slightest redress. It began favourably with his winning the toss; it threatened to go awry when two for 85 quickly became three for 95, at which point Root was a tentative 5. Soon after, with two men back, he took on a short ball from Hazlewood and was harried and hurried into a hook.

It was the kind of early counterattacking shot of which Root made a speciality in 2015. It was the kind of slightly inattentive stroke that cost Root his wicket in Melbourne last week. For an instant, Root's innings, perhaps even his career, hung with that top edge — when it bisected the fielders, he looked suitably penitent. He had faced fifty deliveries before taking advantage of some width from Starc to drive through the covers with that signature of the right knee on the ground. He acknowledged applause for 50 perfunctorily, job not even half done.

This was Root's first Test in Sydney, where four years ago he became part of England's Ashes debris. There was a sense in which his innings here was about four years hence — the opportunity to captain England in Australia again being one he has admitted to coveting, to take advantage of the lessons he has learned this summer.

It was destined as an application to remain incomplete, curtailed by the second new ball.

Boundaries came from Starc's first two deliveries, a booming drive, a sketchy edge; the third, an inviting leg stump half volley, was loosely clipped, well caught and forlornly rued; and so a nineteenth innings elapsed without three figures.

It was hard to be too critical — Root will have hit countless shots like it, and executed them flawlessly. But when England lost Jonny Bairstow in the next over, the day's last, much of day's hard work was squandered.

What chance Root's second opportunity to lead in Australia? He has had some harsh reviews, notably Ricky Ponting's asperities after the Perth Test — that Root captained England like 'a little boy'; that he was 'really quiet and too shy to say too much.'

Truth be told, a losing captain is pressed to say very much at all, beyond falling back on tired lines about 'working hard' and 'moving forward'. At his last press conference, Root sounded less like a boy than a bureaucrat, foreshadowing changes in 'the seam-bowling department' and 'the spin department' as though he had come from HR to pin a note to the bulletin board.

The fact is, too, that much about Root's captaincy future lies, while it's wearisome to repeat it, in the hands of the Crown Prosecution Service. The gap left by Ben Stokes' absence has only grown on this tour; probably some time during the one-day series, when the CPS is tipped to make public its decision, it may gape still further. In that respect, 2021 seems a very long way off.

It was at times a day's hard work for Australia, on a pitch whose green flecks seemed to be fading under the warm sun by the over. There was an edge off the bowling and flaws in the out-cricket, an opportunity to run out a ball-watching Malan going astray. Pat Cummins toiled nobly in his first Test appearance on his home ground, and after nine consecutive Tests is in uncharted physical territory.

For Australia, though, it should have been harder still. And were you looking for reasons the hosts have come out ahead in this series, you might observe that England's top three have remained unchanged despite passing 60 twice in the entire series.

James Vince will commence his twentieth Test innings with two half-centuries to show for it. Yesterday he provided the usual indicators of quality and occasioned the standard pangs of disquiet: flails through cover and over point to take him into the nervous teens; a commanding pull shot to push the needle into the red of the mid-20s, and it is unnecessary to report further. It's almost as though Vince has never been advised that it's permissible to bat for longer: one would write more about him, but he never leaves any more to say. It's more than runs compiled in this series that have decided it; it is also runs forgone.

FREE MASON

5 January 2018

What were you doing at the age of twenty? Maybe you were tackling your first menial job, waiting tables, pulling beers, still having your mother do your washing. Perhaps you were at university, attending the odd lecture, cramming for exams, and wondering where this inevitably mediocre degree would take you. Possibly you were backpacking, or penning bad poetry, or playing in a band, or thinking about a tattoo.

Mason Crane is bowling leg-spin for England. Two years ago he was at school. A year ago he was a spectator at the Sydney Test, whilst playing local grade cricket. Two days ago he posted photographs of himself on Instagram with his proud parents, Harbour Bridge in the background, and his new teammates, receiving a Test cap from Graeme Swann: 'This is my favourite and proudest moment ever!! Truly honoured, I hope we can have a great 5 days. Living my dream.' Plus an emoji or two, which I'm too old to translate.

After a quiet day's dressing room duties, Crane emerged yesterday for his first Test hit. First impressions? With his compact physique and long sleeves, back-and-across step and bat gesturing towards point, he bore a striking resemblance to Steve Smith — not a bad model, all things considered, even if he was not to last long, after a tail end mix-up.

Second impressions? He might bowl a bit like Steve Smith too. Beckoned by Joe Root to bowl the fifteenth over of Australia's reply, Crane started with a drag-down to Usman Khawaja, a ball directed down the leg side to David Warner, and a slightly strained glance at his captain, himself only twenty-seven, and learning his own set of ropes.

This particular rope Root must have known already. Crane's first-class strike rate of 68.2 is barely inferior to Nathan Lyon's of 67.9, but his wickets are almost 10 runs costlier. He will probably always leak runs; captains will have to hope for wickets along the way. Crane cupped and blew into his right hand — an habitual, possibly superstitious gesture — before landing his third ball on a length. There was a burst of sympathetic applause.

Nobody expected Crane to turn the series on its head, England trailing 0-3 already being buried up their necks. But his selection had already provided relief from a tour of demoralising defeat and a veritable covfefe of negative press. The hope now was not so much about what might go right but that too much should not go wrong.

In the final Test of two of the last three Ashes series, England has blooded a slow bowler — neither Simon Kerrigan nor Scott Borthwick were reblooded. As far as leg-spin is concerned, England can look back on Chris Schofield and Ian Salisbury, capped at 21 and 22 respectively, for a cumulative 20 wickets in seventeen Tests.

On the evidence here, although it may not be saying much, Crane already looks a better bowler than all four. He bustles up, whirling busily, rolls his shoulders and rips it. With the initial challenge of two left-handers to bowl to, he maintained a tidy length and game loop. There was the ghost of an appeal, as a leg-break hit Khawaja just outside the line, and the glimpse of a wrong 'un, which Warner dead batted off the back foot. Sweepers on both sides excused his errors of length, although they allowed strike rotation rather too free.

With Moeen bowling at the other end, it was possible to enjoy the improbability of the spectacle: a fresh-faced lad bowling leggies and a bearded Muslim purveying offices to a batsman in a baggy green (Warner) before a packed Test house. Which decade were we in again?

The romance of leg-spin is that its purveyors can cause themselves as much difficulty as their opponents. It is a craft lived in the head and felt in the fingers — and at twenty, of course, mind and body are still maturing. Crane ended up bowling 102 deliveries at batsmen during the day, and probably almost as many again to Alastair Cook at cover, rehearsing and visualising. Thanks for his fields, he struggled to get consecutive deliveries at the same batsmen, conceding 30 singles.

From one particular challenge, Crane emerged well. In his tenth over, he came nearest to a wicket so far, when an edge from Khawaja bisected a baulked keeper and an unsighted slip. Then, twice, he bustled up, only to keep hold of the ball, as though coming up to a neighbourhood door on which he was afraid to knock. When he did, the occupant was hostile: Smith pasted a full pitch through mid-wicket for four.

Crane followed his poorest with his best, continuing to attack in his eleventh over when defence must have seemed tempting: Smith edged a leg-break just short of slip, and Khawaja gloved just out of the reach of both short leg and the on-rushing bowler. And this is not, at least not yet, a surface on which to judge him: in seventy-two overs of spin these first two days, just one wicket has fallen.

As shadows crossed the field after the close, Crane's day concluded with a televised boundary side interrogation by Swann, Mike Hussey and Geoffrey Boycott, nearly 250 Test caps between them. He must have been pinching himself throughout. There's another aspect of his being twenty that should prove unusual — he'll be able to remember it.

A CRY IN THE WILDERNESS

6 January 2018

Cricketers have a standard set of bad dreams. Traditional subjects include dropped catches, scary fast bowlers. A whole sub-genre is concerned with being next in when a wicket falls and being unable to find your bat/gloves/protector/dentures. The hallucination of taking a wicket with a no ball has never, as far as I know, been reported. It may be imminent.

'Living my dream' tweeted Mason Crane on the event of his selection for this Test. Yesterday he experienced a waking nightmare, when he implored his captain Joe Root to review an lbw appeal against Usman Khawaja (132), who had offered no shot to his leg-break.

The naked eye made recourse to the Decision Review System look worth the gamble: ball tracker's parabolae frequently throw up surprises. The front line police, however, allow no latitude, even for maiden Test wickets: thanks, perhaps, to the stylish little cutaway of the heel of his sponsor's boot, no part of it remained behind the front line.

(How long, one wonders, before an enterprising shoemonger affixes a slightly trailing heel to their footwear that slightly lengthens the foot's landing field, in the same way as webbing expands the keeper's catching area?)

It's still uncertain whether the third umpire would have ruled in Crane's favour — although ball tracker duly showed the delivery hitting off stump, there remained the subjective judgement of whether Khawaja was playing a shot, in the event rendered moot. But it still fell into the category, like rather too much English cricket this summer, of avoidable error.

As was quickly pointed out, Crane joined England teammates Ben Stokes, Mark Wood and Tom Curran to cheat themselves of their maiden Test wickets by trespasses recently. And since Big Brother started watching the front line, the annulment of wickets by no balls has become, at least in memory and anecdote, rather less of a rarity — with often weighty consequences.

Overnight, for example, India's Jasprit Bumrah had entreated his captain to review a rejected caught behind appeal against Faf du Plessis in the Test in Cape Town, only to have a foot fault revealed. Bumrah, indeed, is a repeat offender: last year, he vitally spared Pakistan's Fakhar Zaman in the Champions Trophy final at the Oval and Sri Lanka's Upul Tharanga in a one-day international at Dharamsala.

Add to this that umpires since video superintendence have been correspondingly less vigilant about the front line, so that a bowler might be transgressing serially without knowing it, and you have, in effect, accidents waiting to happen.

So why have bowlers not backed off the front line to allow greater margin for error? Partly, perhaps, because pushing it has become a habit. Tom Curran's explanation for his gaffe in Melbourne was that he had just consulted the umpire about the placement of his front foot, and been told it was 'half and half', which he took not as guidance to continue as he was but as licence to stretch for an effort ball.

A further issue, I suspect, is responsibility. Outs come easily in the modern game. Hugely experienced bowlers can blame their ineffective lengths on support staff having failed to urge their correction.

Yet apart from 'zero tolerance' policies at training — an idea that's self-contradictory anyway — there doesn't seem much that coaches can do to prevent no balls, except to repeat *Punch*'s age-old advice for those about to marry: 'Don't.' It is somewhere the bowler has complete autonomy and agency; it's up to him where he places his marker; up to him how close he pushes the line.

When Crane transgressed yesterday, he looked bemused, horrified then finally disgruntled, chuntering away to umpire Kumar Dharmasena. But what business does a bowler coming off a few paces have in bowling no balls? He had overstepped the previous day — a warning he'd failed to heed. Crane has been lavished with support and resources in his brief career, encouraged and even coddled every step of the way, exhorted probably to think positively, not to fret overly about his mistakes. To have to own one of them would, at the very least, have been a novel experience.

But let's be fair also. That Stokes, Wood, Curran and Crane have all been snagged on debut is consistent with inexperience of the unforgiving nature of electronic surveillance.

DRS will only ever be used in televised cricket, which will confine it to the elite game, and really only the elite of that elite. That will make the step up to international cricket the riskiest point in each bowler's career vis a vis the front line, at the precise instant where they need the most luck, but are also most inclined to push that luck in the effort to succeed.

At least Crane had only to wait two and a half hours for the addition of a '1' to his wicket column, having Khawaja nicely stumped by Bairstow just after tea. The cost in time, however, bore heavily on England: a score that much larger and bowlers and fielders that much tireder played to advantage of Mitchell Marsh, who laid on a reverberating bat. Twenty-nine not out from 166 balls last week in Melbourne and 63 not out from 87 this week in Sydney is a batsman transformed.

Crane, meanwhile, fit and young as he is, showed his inexperience: in his 36th over, for example, he beat Marsh with a pitch perfect leg break, then donated a full toss and a half-tracker, both gratefully swatted for four. His habit of aborting his run-up threatened to become what Michael Slater calls an 'internet memo'.

At the point when England might conceivably have been through to the tail had Khawaja been dismissed at the first opportunity, Australia clattered along at four an over, making an outfield conspicuously slow for the preceding eight sessions suddenly seem decidedly small. The visitors' day was twice as successful as their worst of the tour, the third in Perth: they took two wickets rather than one. Truly the stuff of nightmares.

SYDNEY TEST DAY 4

LIFE BEGINS AT 40.87

7 January 2018

A funny, nerdy thing happened surreptitiously to Shaun Marsh at the Sydney Cricket Ground yesterday. His Test average, which at the start of this summer inhabited the sleepy groves of the mid-30s, entered the sunny uplands of the low 40s — indeed, when he perished to a run out for 156, it was glowing healthily at 40.87.

For a modern Test batsman, life rather begins at 40: it's the statistical equivalent of the age of consent. Even in this age where Steve Smith seems bent on proving 60 to be the new 50, how you stand in relation to 40.00 has a pronounced influence on your entitlement to batting stature. It's entirely arbitrary, of course, that 40.1 should seem so much heartier than 39.9. But, then, nobody disputes the similar chasm of meaning between the scores 101 and 99.

For most accomplished batsmen, an average of 40 is a floor, which they proceed to reinforce, carpet and upholster to the best of their abilities. Shaun Marsh has crept up the stairs from the storey beneath wearing his socks: at one stage six years ago, despite his entering Test cricket with the fanfare of a debut century, his Test average dwindled to less than 30.

Between times, to put it mildly, Marsh has been a frustrating batsman — frustrating to his advocates no less than to his detractors. His qualities and flaws, being interpretations of the same data, are a matter of perspective.

Marsh crafts quality hundreds, albeit that he has rather spread these out: twenty-four in seventeen years of first-class cricket is a study in gradualism. He has built outstanding partnerships, to win a Test with Steve Smith in Port Elizabeth in 2014, to save a Test with Peter Handscomb in Bengaluru in 2017. He has also formed part of some sorry subsidences, averaging 25.5 in Australian defeats.

Supporters accent the peaks, critics the valleys. He looks the part, the former have said. He *looks* the part, the latter have replied. The supporters, who include the important ones of his national coach Darren Lehmann and state coach Justin Langer, have had a satisfying summer, culminating yesterday in the 34-year-old's second century of these Ashes. Only James Anderson caused Marsh any discomfort, causing him to nick between first and second slip, then twice to play at thin, enervatingly hot air. The threat soon evaporated, as it were.

It was an innings built for purpose too. As brother Mitchell took 101 out of their 200-minute partnership of 169, there was no mistaking that Shaun's support was fraternal as well as professional. Sporting manlove is a modern commonplace, but the pair enriched theirs with a special spontaneity by not waiting until they had completed their second run to embrace, dancing a delighted circle round one another in a veritable Philadelphia of brotherly jubilation. Under similar circumstances, the Chappells might have mumbled beneath their moustaches and the Waughs exchanged a reflex nod.

Fitting in is what Shaun Marsh has always rather struggled to do. At the simplest level, he has always been coming and going, form and fitness being responsible for no fewer than eight starts and re-starts in his international career.

Perhaps what has changed this season has not only been him. A challenge for Marsh is that he has never been exactly the batsman that Australia has been looking for. They have not been seeking a daintily elegant left-hander who hits a sweet cover drive and clips crisply off the toes. They have been seeking replacements for Ponting, Clarke, Hayden, Langer, Martyn et al.

Australian batting in the last decade has been a story of holes and roles, with Shaun Marsh having enjoyed a run at all of them: his 49 Test innings have been spread across eight different slots in Australia's order. And that Australia has come back to him so often has reflected a paucity of alternatives. This summer, however, Marsh has found a niche, starting the series at number six, then moved up one slot to accommodate his brother. Is this his best position? Maybe that matters less than after whom he is batting. With Steve Smith in millennium-defining form, coming in next is the best seat in the house.

In the Smith era, funnily enough, Marsh is a slightly quaint pleasure to watch — a sort of anti-Smith in his simplicity of method and absence of mannerism, except for a wafting top-handed leave outside off stump, like a kind of sword trick. He stands and plays, does not leave you wondering how he does it — only, frustratingly, that he doesn't always.

Coming in ahead of your younger brother must also rank high among cricket pleasures. We shall learn more of the partnership in South Africa in March, when the wickets are not so flat and the ball is no longer going gun barrel straight, but they have done all and more that could be expected of them here.

It was so much Marsh's day that it hardly mattered when he dropped Alastair Cook to his right at first slip, for Cook consumed only ten more deliveries. James Vince, meanwhile, has become to the English an inferior version of what Marsh used to be to Australians. Perhaps every country needs one.

There have been some delays, detours and distractions, but what was left yesterday was disparity, between that no Englishman had a good day and no Australian had a bad day. A few other landmarks loomed too. For stats geeks out there, Tim Paine averages 39.91.

SYDNEY TEST DAY 5

VIN ORDINAIRE

8 January 2018

Prediction in sport has the curious quality of giving the greatest pleasure when it is mistaken. When a favourite loses, a champion falters, or for the books there is a good old turn-up, one has usually seen something out of the ordinary, inspiring, memorable.

A feature of these Ashes — a feature that arguably should disturb us — is how closely it followed the prophecies. Certain players did better and worse than expected. But the trends and issues were all long-term talking points. Hot takes? You'd find hotter in an RSL bain-marie.

To the victor the spoils. Australia have shown what it takes to win here: surgical strikes with the new ball, precision accuracy with the old, first innings runs based around big hundreds, which might well soon be called 'Smiths'. They were fortunate to stay fit, of course, although that's not just the work of providence.

Much of this, furthermore, could have been written and sealed in a time capsule before a ball was bowled. The known knowns were that Australia, with three excellent fast bowlers and a world-class slow bowler, enjoyed an overpowering advantage on their own surfaces; that England, without their number one player, would find it immensely difficult to take twenty wickets with the Kookaburra, and had their best opportunity to sneak a win in the test tube environment of Adelaide under lights.

Even then, the man-for-man comparisons were accented by intervening daylight — that Australia's number three averaged twice as much as England's number three; that England's first-choice spinner paid twice as much for his wickets away as Australia's at home. How were these gaps to be bridged? Not by stringing a rope ladder of hope across them.

Some have called this series reminiscent of English cricket's 'bad old days' two decades ago. Yet one had to wonder after a time: were these quite so bad? After all, in both 1994-5 and 1998-9, the series were live going into the final Tests. More series like this one, and we'll be writing of the *belle époque* of the De Freitas Years.

Actually, England were luckier than they deserved. The fourth day in Sydney apart, summer has been mild — as mild, in fact, as when England bucked the twenty-first century trend seven years ago and retained the Ashes on tour. Steven Finn aside, the visitors suffered no significant injuries or impairments, and were able to choose from their full squad in every game but the last, when Chris Woakes could probably have played had it been absolutely necessary. James Anderson stayed fit all summer, and at thirty-five got through more overs in a series than ever before. Amazing to say, James Vince made 83 at the Gabba, at which point he should have been sold like Bitcoin.

Joe Root called correctly four times, and lost all four Tests. Had Root been unlucky at the toss, we might by now have been deploring the ritual as an anachronism, opining on why choice of innings should be granted visiting captains etc. As it was, England's fate recalled Australia's in the 2013 Border-Gavaskar Trophy: four won tosses, four first innings, four complete pizzlings.

Perversely, the malarkey about off-field carousing probably did England as much good as harm: if you believed in it, it provided an explanation ('Unprofessional'; 'Behaving like university students'); if you didn't, it engaged your sympathy at the coverage's unfairness ('Boys will be boys'; 'Aussie media cheerleaders'). Did it unsettle the visitors? It could just as easily have unified them. Who knows or cares? Sober, drunk, united or disunited, England were simply inferior.

You get the sense that England, more particularly old Australia hands like Anderson, Stuart Broad, Alastair Cook and their coach Trevor Bayliss, knew this all along — that their strategy was chiefly to hang in there as long as possible, to keep defeat within margins acceptable to England Cricket Board management. Certainly the praise lavished on Root for his Yorkshire Wall field placements at Brisbane looks in hindsight like the approval of the defensive strategies of Andre Maginot.

In all honesty, this was a middling-to-mediocre Ashes series, longer on individual achievement than on drama and event, loyally watched by large crowds but after Perth agonizingly drawn out. Australia performed its tasks efficiently and effectively if unspectacularly. Their pace bowling was wonderfully disciplined. Nathan Lyon was consistently threatening. But there was no Mitchell Johnson to provide edge-of-the-seat thrills, no Kevin Pietersen to provide a recognizable anti-Aussie.

The rhetoric was routinely vacuous, with England providing press conference after press conference of insistences that they had played well at times, that the scoreline did not reflect the differences between the teams, that bowlers had been unlucky to beat the bat, that batsmen had been victims of deliveries that would have defeated God. It became as convincing as Theresa May droning and sniffling about the 'British Dream' while letters fell from her backdrop.

Mind you, speaking of backdrops, Cricket Australia's marketing department set new standards with the retro wheeze of holding yesterday's presentation on what looked like an old Moomba float constructed from the polystyrene packed around whitegoods, with an Australian hand holding up four fingers and an English hand clenched in a remonstrating fist (Ben Stokes', perhaps).

The players squatted in front of a big cut-out Ashes urn while sparklers guttered like candles on a kids' birthday cake. The scoreboard then asked spectators to 'leave in a safe manner'. Look out Superbowl! If there an ICC code of conduct for presentations, this would have incurred a three-point penalty ('Crap'). The series deserved better. Although maybe not hugely better.

THE ASHES NOW

SOOT?

9 January 2018

There is cricket in Australia, and there is Ashes cricket. It has its own history and tradition, specifications and tonnage. England may not provide our best opposition, but there is no doubt that it is our favourite.

As much as has changed about Australian summers in the last decade, the primacy of the Ashes has again this summer proven immutable. The 867,000 clicks the turnstile were the second most ever, and the biggest postwar. Daily television ratings have been between three and five million. Social content ratings into the hundreds of thousands of interactions made it more than twice as popular as any other sport.

Funnily enough, the series also set records for slowness of scoring, England essentially trying to run the siege that it was under. If you like Steve Smith, it was like tuning in to one of those pop-up pay-TV channels for *Star Trek* marathons — on and on he went, boldly going as no batsman since Bradman had gone before as a hardcore audience watched transfixed.

Interestingly, crowds in the new juggernaut, the T20 Big Bash League, have come off their peaks by about a tenth this summer, having shown signs in preceding years of cannibalising international crowds. They may pick up now the series is over, but there is a limit to the number of games of cricket a family can attend in the course of summer, as commendably straightforward and cheap as attendance has been made.

Spare a thought for visitors who have come a long way, as some of them would say, for nowt. Since the Barmy Army struck its colours, England has won one series in Australia out of seven, and this summer did not even have a favourable exchange rate, 58p to the dollar being a far cry from the halcyon days of 2002-3 celebrated in song ('We're fat, we're round/Three dollars to the pound'). England's three overseas victories since Trevor Bayliss became coach in May 2015 must by now be testing a few tourism budgets. The England Cricket Board might be throwing everything at white ball cricket, but that's a crummy sport to follow on the road.

And make no mistake, England this summer were never very good and often quite poor — with their all-right-on-the-night selections and hang-on-by-the-fingernails strategies, they resembled at times not so much an England team as an England team tribute band, an inferior copy, with, as they say in these parts, all of the gear but no idea. In his *Pietersen on Cricket*,

Kevin Pietersen averred: 'For an England player there's no more intimidating place than Australia.' This team made it seem all that and more.

Yet perhaps that's one of the reasons Australians go on thinking that too much Ashes cricket is not enough — the sense of personal connectedness to their team is strongest when they are pitted against England. Cricket Australia's #BeatEngland hashtag may have scaled the north face of peak stupid, but what was notable was that #BeatIndia, #BeatNewZealand, #BeatZimbabwe or whatever would have made no sense at all.

There, indeed, is the rub. The Ashes has been so successful vis-à-vis the rest of Test cricket, it has grown like a cornerstone very nearly as large as the building. This success is a mixed blessing, for it shows up the paucity of other significant bilateral rivalries, even as we approach a system that from next year will decide the majority of these rivalries over the distance of two Tests.

The International Cricket Council's mooted Test Championship is based on the idea of bringing context from outside. Yet the lesson of the Ashes is that the most valuable, enriching and irreplaceable context is generated from within: it lifts cricket above the quality of the spectacle. Never mind that these five Ashes Tests were rarely exhilarating, sometimes austere, occasionally quite dull. They drew an authenticity from antiquity, a quality from continuity. Another quest should be for finding meaning in the cricket we already play — and if the ICC had its wits about it, it could go a long way to reviving Test cricket at a single stroke.

Last month marked a decade since the last time India and Pakistan met in a Test match, at Bengaluru. The rivalry at the time was red hot — India's victory over Pakistan in the World T20 final had touched off the revolution in the short game whose fullest expression is the Indian Premier League. Since then, apart from their occasional encounters in ICC events, they have met in only one bilateral one-day series, the deterioration in their nation's relationship beginning with the Lashkar-e-Taiba attacks on the city of Mumbai in November 2008 and the Lashkar-e-Jhangvi attacks on the Sri Lankan team bus in Lahore in March 2009, further aggravated by the rise of Hindu chauvinism. There was talk of the restoration of ties around the time of the Big 3 carve-up of world cricket, but it went by the board — or, to be more precise, boards, of India and Pakistan, who are now in the early stages of legal action. The result is foreordained: Lawyers 1, Cricket 0.

Sometimes it is thought that given the thrall of the Ashes, it might be expedient to play it more often: thus the experiment, entirely idiotic, of ten consecutive Ashes Tests in 2013-14. Test cricket does not need any more Ashes. But it could do with more of Ashes-like 'feeling'. Even at a neutral venue, an absorbing, well-tempered Test series between India and Pakistan would be unbelievable box office. It might even put Ashes cricket in the shade. And that would be entirely a good thing.

PITCHES

GARBAGE IN, GARBAGE OUT

10 January 2018

Returning to Melbourne from Sydney on Tuesday afternoon, my first port of call was naturally the nets at the cricket club where I've played these last twenty-five years: after all, mediocrity needs constant reinforcement. The good news was that all the talk was of a Test match; the bad news was that the Test match concerned was not here.

No, the chat was of South Africa versus India at Newlands, which started with Bhuvaneshwar Kumar swinging it round corners, and ended with Vernon Philander doing the same. Eighteen wickets in a day. No centuries, but some brilliant counterattacking batsmanship on a roller rink of an outfield. Brave captaincy from Faf du Plessis and Virat Kohli. 'Just as an advert for Test cricket, that's as good as it gets,' said du Plessis. 'There was no boring Test cricket, it was a lot of action. And that's why we absolutely loved this Test match.'

Meanwhile in Australia, two cheers for the Ashes was about what they deserved. There were fine individual performances and incidental pleasures, and splendid collective purpose among the winners. Yet would anyone have called it an 'advert for Test cricket'? Could you work up a 'love' for the lowest Ashes scoring rates since 1994-95 and two dead Tests, the former afflicted with rigor mortis.

The big difference, of course, were conditions underfoot. In Cape Town, both captains called the pitch 'outstanding'. Yet the biggest men's and women's games of the Australian summer were protracted draws on drop-in pitches not so much dull as lobotomised. The Melbourne Cricket Ground produced a pitch that did not change in a week; North Sydney Oval offered a surface that might as well have been synthetic.

There were pedestrian stretches of play on permanent wicket blocks too. On one day at the WACA Ground, a single wicket fell; on one day at the Sydney Cricket Ground, two. Brisbane's Test has turned into an annual anti-climax, not so much Gabbatoir as Gabbatoilet, all tennis ball bounce and concrete pillbox architectural charm.

To be fair there were a couple of exciting days at the WACA before it flattened out, then later when its cracks opened, along with the novelty of rain. And Adelaide Oval, with the additional thatch for the sake of the pink ball, showed drop-ins in a decidedly favourable light. But the biggest and most storied ground in Australia did not produce a result in a first-class match last year. Last year!

There are limits to what figures can tell us in this area. Aggregate batting statistics are inherently volatile. It doesn't necessarily follow that Zimbabwe is a hard place to bat; the team batting most often there is Zimbabwe. But some salient facts in an analysis by Ric Finlay are worth reporting. In 2000, despite us having a team of the talents, Australia was one of tougher places in the world to bat. Test batsmen worldwide were making 29.44 runs per wicket; in Australia it was 27.84. For the next decade, as you'd expect, we bobbed around either side of that world average, sometimes above, sometimes below.

The last six years, though, we've been above it; in the last four years, runs have come more readily here than anywhere in the world. The global average has risen to 33.47; in Australia, despite sometimes flakey line-ups, the average has been 38.81, higher even than on the grassless, paceless clay in the UAE.

These differences might not seem huge, but sustained over every wicket and every innings for a whole year implies a worsening balance between bat and ball — which, funnily enough, Cricket Australia's James Sutherland opined in Melbourne was 'incredibly important to the future of Test cricket'.

He's right. The fundamental problem with flat pitch cricket is that momentum is all-but irretrievable if lost. Instead of glorious uncertainty, you can turn the television off for five hours and guess the score within ten per cent when you turn it back on — which, frankly, was the case a lot of this summer. It narrows the skills that can succeed. It conduces to long stretches of not much.

So how did this happen? The advance of drop-ins seem only part of the story. Grounds themselves are changing. Towering stands have altered their microclimates. Drainage is markedly improved from the era when a shower ruined a day's cricket, and a day's rain turned footballers into mudlarks — a counterpart to John O'Gready's famous photograph of Provan and Summons is unimaginable today. Squares no longer retain water as they used to. Flecked with green on the first day, Sydney's pitch rolled out biscuit brown on the second.

Regional differences were once pronounced and abiding. When the SCG was coming into use as an Australian rules football stadium for the Sydney Swans in the 1980s, a team meeting at rival Geelong considered how to approach its wide wings and deep pockets. So, asked coach Malcolm Blight, how did the players think they should tackle the SCG? 'Play two spinners,' responded centre half forward Billy Brownless.

Nowadays, the small Australian curatorial community shares intelligence and encourages conservatism and uniformity. After all, who wants to cost their boss gate takings in the event of a three-day Test? Bellerive Oval hosted the last match of that kind — actually a pretty exciting game, which Steve Smith credits with being 'the making of me as a captain' by exposing him to character-forming adversity. But Hobart has now lost its Test to Canberra, where Manuka Oval provides a pitch of suitably parliamentary monotony.

Another contributing factor was the Argus review which when rolled out to scare Australian cricket straight reported 'a significant amount of unfavourable commentary' on local pitches, felt too skewed to obtaining results. That's an aspect of cricket culture often remarked on — everyone feels good when there are centuries being scored. Flat track bullies making tons of runs also suits a bureaucracy obsessed with measurement, being quantifiable and orderly. When cricket accommodates a variety of skills, incorporates risk, opens unforeseen possibilities, then it's all a bit of a danger to KPIs.

We're now encountering the second-order effects of Australia's flat wicket culture, which is the obsession with everyone bowling in the range of 140-150kmh. Said coach Darren Lehmann this week: 'In Australia you need velocity, you need pace, it's simple — history shows that.' No it isn't, and no it doesn't. Tysons and Thomsons are outliers. Ray Lindwall and Dennis Lillee were great bowlers, not simply fast bowlers; Glenn McGrath won many more Tests for Australia at 135kmh than Brett Lee at 150kmh.

This newly received wisdom that Tests require 200cm automata bowling 145kmh, and that this is cool because we have got them and others don't, bespeaks a narrow-minded and self-defeating fortress Australia mentality that is antagonistic to the future of Test cricket.

Time for a change. This wealthy game is good at getting others to pick up the tab. Decision Review System? Up to the broadcasters. Pink ball? Over to you, Kookaburra. Pitches? Why not invest in improving their variety and vitality, even in leading the world in drop-in technology, if that is, indeed, the future? That way we might lose the odd Test; but that way we might also have something to talk about.

THE KERRY PACKER MEDAL

DÉTENTE

19 January 2018

You can still visit it at Cricket Australia's website. A few keystrokes take you to space set aside for results from the Australia A tour of South Africa that was scheduled for 12 July to 8 August 2017.

Instead, there are three rather forlorn news stories, and two photographs of captain Usman Khawaja: in his baggy green, and in his suit next to officials of the Australian Cricketers' Association announcing on 2 July that the selected players would decline to tour while the bulk of the country's senior male and female cricketers were out of contract with CA.

To this last week was added a footnote, albeit unlikely to feature on cricket.com.au. In its newsletter *Onside*, the association executive announced that Khawaja and his squad had been unanimously voted winners of the Kerry Packer Award for 'those deemed to have served the ACA in an outstanding capacity.'

Simon Katich, the award's last recipient, joining a lineage including former presidents Darren Lehmann and Ian Healy, and chief executives Tim May and Paul Marsh, called their decisions 'courageous', 'selfless' and engendering 'incredible respect'.

Piquantly, none of the twenty players were identified, not even Khawaja, although their names are easy enough to find: among those who forsook the trip's four-day leg, a prized opportunity for players in the Ashes frame, were Glenn Maxwell, Hilton Cartwright, Travis Head and Kurtis Patterson.

Yet some delicacy is understandable. Six months since the tour that never was, there's reticence about letting anything impinge on the summer that is. It has been in this sense a healing summer, efforts of players and administrators channelled into the Ashes goal. CA have completed their private internal review of the negotiation, chairman David Peever reporting in from his parallel universe by brushing off criticism of the belated involvement of his CEO James Sutherland: 'You have to bear in mind James runs a very large organisation, a large, complex organisation, and he's time-poor.' Up to a point, Lord Peever.

There has been talk of social fraternisation between CA directors and the ACA executive. In three weeks, the parties will jointly stage the Allan Border Medal, which hardly seemed a certainty when the parties could hardly sit in the same room together at periods in the negotiation.

All the same, sources of tension remain. Personnel at the organisations have not changed. There have been low-level irritations, such as CA's release of a five-year strategic plan that left the ACA unmentioned, while Big Bash League over rate fines and penalties have smacked of a policy of pinpricks.

The ACA has also been taking stock of itself through activities marking the imminent twentieth anniversary of the first memorandum of understanding — a deal, not unlike last year's, preceded by more than a year of argy-bargy.

It's striking in hindsight that Australian players, after missing their first opportunity to unionise in the wake of World Series Cricket, went on being paid so poorly so long, under arrangements where they were dealt with individually on a take-it-or-leave-it basis. Even after Mark Taylor piled up 839 runs in the 1989 Ashes series, his retainer contract with the Australian Cricket Board was $9000. It was Taylor, by then Australian captain, who called off spinner May, a chartered accountant, suggesting he might take on the task of acting as the players' industrial representative.

The context was the AFL Players' Association's successful fight for recognition by the Australian Football League in 1993, followed by the formation of the Australian Soccer Players' Association and the advent of Super League. In his advocacy of a collective bargaining agreement involving a fixed proportion of revenue, May did something still more remarkable. He did not merely call on the players' allegiance to one another, but their sense of intergenerational solidarity — quite a stretch of imagination. In his autobiography, Steve Waugh quotes from an ACA newsletter where May enjoined members to think of 'future generations of cricketers': 'Don't let them down, don't let yourselves down. Stay with this together, and you will win and win well.'

Ironically, the individual who broke ranks was Taylor, who in a famous vote during a WACA Test against New Zealand using a baggy green as a ballot box, was the lone holdout against strike action — and who last year, of course, was securely ensconced on the CA board and the Nine commentary box. Funny how things work out.

Looking back on last year, it may be the endurance of this collective conscience that's most surprising. The determination to stick by one another, to not surrender rights that predecessors fought for, to even look after those predecessors by the funding of welfare programmes, was proved to have survived into an era that exalts the individual, cocoons the elite, and finds annual expression in the financial orgy of the Indian Premier League auction.

The abiding question is whether this will last the ACA's next twenty years and longer. To next Saturday's sale, IPL franchises will bring kitties of $16 million. To the next generation, cricketers will bring a different set of backgrounds, having been nurtured, so to speak, within cricket 'systems' and 'markets' rather than 'teams' and 'communities'. The pay dispute gave cricketers a feeling of what they can accomplish collectively; there remain lots of exogenous forces dividing them.

How far can their loyalties extend even now? After the Sydney Test, there was a meeting of the Marylebone Cricket Club's World Cricket Committee, whose members include not only Ricky Ponting and Kumar Sangakkara but also the unflagging May — if he ever got round to them, incidentally, TBA's memoirs would be well worth reading.

Among its recommendations was 'some form of minimum wage and payment structure' to 'close the gap and the present imbalance in international cricket.' There's the rub: 'some form'. Nobody knows what this looks like, how it might be mandated, and who might have to give something up.

Paradoxically, the rise of domestic T20 has also acted as a blender of experiences and backgrounds. Cricketers have never been more aware of the challenges facing their brothers and sisters in other lands. But in the end, tackling issues requires individuals to be like the members of that Australia A squad and look past their immediate self-interest. It was Packer himself who thought that a touch of the harlot lurked in us all.

GLENN MAXWELL

DAMNED IF HE DOES

26 January 2018

Glenn Maxwell is a fascinating cricketer. It is not, at the moment, doing him much good.

He is fascinating for how he plays, for the spontaneity and daring with which he deploys an astonishing repertoire of strokes, and for his sheer versatility: only one other Australian has made a hundred in each of the three international formats. He is fascinating, too, for how the reactions he engenders reveal his surroundings, and offer a kind of commentary on them.

Alongside David Warner, Maxwell is the talent most closely associated with the rise of T20 in this country. Yet while Warner has prostrated himself obediently before the Test altar, part of Maxwell remains untamed, and in certain eyes somehow unreliable.

This is a big week in Maxwell's career. It has begun with his exclusion from the Test squad to tour South Africa, six weeks after he was, as the reserve batsman at the Gabba, considered in the country's best seven bats, and in spite of his being, between times, the Sheffield Shield's leading runmaker and the highest and fastest scorer at his Big Bash League franchise. It will conclude this weekend with involvement in the Indian Premier League auction, where Maxwell was bought for $US1 million as long as five years ago, where last year he captained Kings XI Punjab, and where he is perhaps more liked and lauded than in Australia.

It follows a catalogue of mixed messages and drive-by sledges dating back to December 2016 when Maxwell called down a disproportionate wrath by remarking that at a press conference it was 'a little bit painful' to be batting behind his keeper-captain Matthew Wade for Victoria and opining that he 'might have been a chance' for a Test call-up.

This violated the great press conference taboo on providing other than confirmation that the boys done well and were trying 110 per cent. Maxwell was fined an undisclosed amount according to an undisclosed code by a hitherto veiled Australian 'team leadership group' for being 'very disrespectful', as Steve Smith explained not in an official deliberation but in his column for Cricket Australia's website.

Into the bargain, coach Darren Lehmann scoffed at Maxwell's selection prospects: 'Are you going to pick a bloke who hasn't made a hundred in two years?' In actual fact Maxwell had, despite his first-class opportunities being constrained by his international one-day duties — in 2014-15, for example, Maxwell had a single Sheffield Shield innings batting at number seven, preparatory to averaging 65 and striking at 182 in the World Cup.

It's true that Maxwell's fifty-over performances had tapered steadily post the Cup, but his T20 performances in the preceding six months had remained outstanding: an average of 61, a strike rate of 178. Additional oddity lay in those chosen for the Test team in Maxwell's stead: first Nic Maddinson, with a first-class average bobbing around in the mid-30s, then Mitchell Marsh, with a first-class average in his preceding score of games of less than 20. Opportunity came only when the latter succumbed to injury in India, whereupon Maxwell scored a match-saving maiden Test hundred at Ranchi, and top-scored in the second innings of the subsequent defeat at Dharamsala.

The acutest contrast, of course, is with Shaun Marsh, whose treatment over the years has been everything's Maxwell has not: a chorus of golden opinions and uninterrupted boosterism from selectors and coaches alike, which at length has borne fruit this summer. But the opportunities could just as easily have been Maxwell's. In four away Tests last year, Maxwell's average was twice the older Marsh's; in three Shield games before the Gabba Test, Maxwell's average was also superior. Sure, averages are indicative rather than definitive. Yet when chairman of selectors Trevor Hohns announced Marsh's preferment in mid-November, he failed even to mention the fact of Maxwell's omission.

Subsequently Maxwell has been dismissed with banalities. He should make 'big hundreds' — as opposed to small? He should be 'more consistent' — as opposed to less? Hard to keep pace with these dazzling insights, isn't it? The latest is that he should 'train a little bit smarter' — as opposed, presumably, to a little bit dumber?

What Smith meant by the last of these is anyone's guess. Some say that at practice Maxwell gets out too often; some say that at practice he prefers to avoid pointless peppering by fast bowlers; some say that … but why say anything? For heaven's sake, it's practice. Not everyone approaches practice with identical objectives. Not everyone wants, like Smith, to smash throwdowns compulsively until the coaches' arms are falling off. Some just want to feel bat on ball, to build confidence, even — amazing to say — to have fun. Maxwell is twenty-nine. He has played cricket successfully all over the world. If he has a preferred method of preparation, especially in an age when Australia has more personnel in the back room than the dressing room, why not accommodate it? 'Everyone the same' is for cults not cricket teams.

The maverick talent poses an abiding challenge to cricket, a team game involving mutuality, planning and lots of waiting. Trevor Bayliss offered Ben Stokes the carrot of permission and indulgence, with great short-term success, and tougher medium-term consequences. But the stick, and the emergent Australian fetish for promoting insecurity in the name of stimulating competition, makes less sense than ever, especially when it is possible for players to choose cultures more congenial.

Which brings us to this weekend. There's a residual attitude in Australia that a player could only ever be going to the IPL for money. If this ever held it does no longer. An appeal of the domestic T20 leagues around the world, in fact, is their flexibility and diversity. Cultures are less rigid, more fluid, and arguably more adult. Sometimes the results are negative, chaotic, with the mercy that one has only to cop it for so long. But sometimes it's great, because it feels self-created, and because the avid pursuit of T20 formulae promotes an atmosphere of freedom, opportunity and experiment.

The life of the T20 freelancer is innately precarious and potentially lonely. But is it any more so than being one out against a top-heavy, non-negotiable, one-sizes-fits-all cricket system? Perhaps it will not be Glenn Maxwell — he seems laudably desperate to represent his country. But at some stage, I suspect we face the prospect of players opting out of our national set-up not for more money but for less bullshit.

AUSTRALIA IN SOUTH AFRICA
CRICKET MADIBA-STYLE

23 February 2018

The modern cricket tour can be a monotonous affair: congested schedules, restricted interactions, planned to the minute, budgeted to the shekel. Yet South Africa, where Australia commences a four-Test series on Thursday, continues offering the visiting player and pundit something different, more alien, more intense.

Australia's relations with South Africa are of a looser weave than with, say, England, India or New Zealand. Our players are not drawn there by counties or franchises. Our quadrennial visits seldom feature on free-to-air television.

Despite this, Australia has a habit of touring South Africa at seminal moments, since our first visit, just months after the Boer War. Lindsay Hassett's team of 1949 found the first planks of apartheid being laid; Bill Lawry's team of 1970 was the last to visit during the existence of that iniquitous system.

Twenty-four years later, Allan Border's team toured on the eve of black majority rule, and found the environment ahead of Nelson Mandela's election to be rather heart-in-mouth. Steve Waugh's diary interrupted the deadpan everyday with flashes of candour: 'Most of the team have the feeling that something dreadful will happen shortly, and, to be honest, we cannot wait to get out of the country before such carnage erupts.' Such is contemporary fear and loathing around security, it's possible that a tour under similar circumstances today would not take place.

As it is, Steve Smith's team arrived last week at a point of promise, however temporary it may prove, with Mandela's former protégé Cyril Ramaphosa newly in office after Jacob Zuma's locust presidency. Faf du Plessis's Proteas, too, have become a proud hold out in an increasingly contrived and constructed cricket world.

Cricket identities mean ever less — a parade of slicked-up logos and eye-gashing colours whose superficial differences disguise their uniformity of intent. Designers of England's planned T20 competition recently announced that their franchise names will bear no locations at all, on grounds that freedom from geographic association makes for simpler selling and scheduling. International teams increasingly exhibit the characteristics of, alternatively, the operating units of bureaucracies (Australia), the personality cults of star players (India), the rag-tag remnants of former glory (West Indies) and the sufferers of eternal exile (Pakistan). The Proteas are an exception, looking every time they take the field like a genuine, even passionate, expression of their nation — something accentuated by cricket being for so long the preserve of the country's white minority, and despite South African patriotism being so culturally complicated.

Cricket South Africa's latest initiative is to surf the surge in sentiment stirred by the universally empowering milestone of Mandela's centenary this August.

South Africa's recent Test series with India was played for no less than the Mandela-Gandhi Trophy — analogous to an Anglo-American sporting competition for the Churchill-Roosevelt Cup, but reinforced by it being a century and a quarter in May since Gandhi's famous radicalisation at Pietermaritzburg (when he was expelled from a train for being dark-skinned). There is something truly soul stirring about watching Kagiso Rabada and Vernon Philander steam in, Temba Bavuma and Khaya Zondo step forward, and Lungi Ngidi and Junior Dala step up.

For those years when the Proteas were at their best on the road, there were murmurings about an inhibiting burden of local expectation. Lately that has lifted somewhat: defeat by India at Wanderers three weeks ago was the Proteas' first in a home Test for more than two years.

South Africa's challenges are no less unique. The cricket economy is tenuous. Cricket South Africa employs roughly the same number of first-class players as Cricket Australia, but on turnover a fifth as large. Racial selection quotas long a feature of the South African game are ever more ambitious, no longer as general as preferment for non-white players but specifically targeting the advancement of the black Africans who represent four-fifths of the population. Belief in their principle is in constant danger of erosion by their practice. The clumsy last-minute replacement by half-fit Philander of in-form Kyle Abbott in the last World Cup semi-final very nearly cost the Proteas the services of a disillusioned AB de Villiers. Nor does player drain that cost South Africa the likes of Kevin Pietersen, Jonathan Trott, Grant Elliott and Neil Wagner shows sign of abating. No fewer than thirty-nine South Africans have become Kolpak players in English county cricket, including the aforementioned Abbott. Then there is the siren song of the world's T20 leagues. No fewer than fifty-seven South Africans featured in the IPL auction, where Rabada and Ngidi joined de Villiers and Du Plessis in the big money stakes.

Contrast this with the paralysis in South Africa since the collapse of its jazzed-up, private-capital T20 Global League, launched with a fanfare a year ago but postponed last October, perhaps indefinitely, when broadcasters shrugged and franchise owners quailed. That left Cricket South Africa without a CEO and still running the nondescript T20 Ram Slam, which itself has been marred by the taint of corruption (suspensions were imposed last year on eight players for varying degrees of consorting with fixers after a report never made public, perhaps from angst at the conspicuous involvement of black Africans, including former internationals Thami Tsolekille and Lonwabo Tsotsobe).

Relations between CSA and the players' South African Cricketers' Association, moreover, have chilled. Though only two months remain of the parties' current memorandum of understanding, which allots players about 23 per cent of annual forecast revenue, CSA's negotiation strategy has been to indulge in Cricket Australia-style brinkmanship — strangely oblivious as to how this turned out for Cricket Australia. Interesting times.

Aside from the injuries to Bavuma and Dale Steyn, the Proteas should start their series against Australia close to full strength, having this summer already disposed of the world's Test number one, India. Du Plessis is a steely leader; his ranks are long on character as well as talent.

But beyond next year's World Cup, which the Proteas will pursue desperately in light of their sorry record in International Cricket Council events, South African cricket's future seems a great deal less certain. A risk is that by the time Australia returns in 2021-22, it could well be just another tour, only worse.

DURBAN TEST

WINNING UGLY

7 March 2018

Umpires in Australia have been known to refer to the Sydney Test effect, whereby the last Test of each southern summer is almost always the unruliest. Players are tired and tetchy. Opponents are sick of one another. Grievances have accumulated and opportunities are dwindling. 'The line' — that hoary Australian invention setting behaviour curbs — starts to blur and warp.

The effect this season was not to be seen — the Ashes had no embers left to stir. But there were hints during the First Test in Kingsmead that the effect had been rolled over, into summer's last tour rather than its last Test. Australia beat South Africa handily, by 115 runs, continuing a cycle of six wins and a draw in their last seven Tests. The first round in what could be a stirring duel for reverse swing was won conclusively by Mitchell Starc, who swerved the ageing Kookaburra round corners in taking nine wickets.

Yet nobody afterwards was looking that happy, required as they were to fend off questions about a stairwell confrontation between David Warner and Quinton de Kock at tea on the fourth day, CCTV footage of which was leaked to a local news outlet, and which quickly circled the globe. No blows were exchanged, but in tone and tenor it bore more than a little resemblance to the eerie scenes that CCTV captured of Ben Stokes's Bristol rampage six months ago.

The Australians had set the scene for a tense Test match in Durban with an insistence that stump mics be faded, muting on-field exchanges. Warner then played the whole Test with a confrontational air. The stairwell encounter followed a particularly willing session in which he celebrated his mercurial run out of AB de Villiers by jeering at partner Aiden Markram — he looked like one of those faces in a mob on the brink of violence. To the wicket that brought de Kock — hard to imagine what comic opportunities were offered by that name really.

Did de Kock complain to the umpires? That inference might be drawn from a boundary side effects mic that overheard Warner calling de Kock a 'fucking sook' as the players headed for the stairwell. The Australians now allege huffily that de Kock crossed 'the line' by saying something 'personal' to Warner as they ascended the steps, as though calling someone a 'fucking sook' was not. The difference, in Australian sensibilities, is that de Kock apparently referred to an unhappy incident in the past of Warner's wife Candice. Others, however, simply see the biter bit, and without much to complain of.

Left out of account, I cannot help thinking, is that Sydney effect. In the last half-year, Australia's vice-captain has played eight Tests, ten one-day internationals, seven T20 internationals and three further first-class matches in five different countries. The burden is exacerbated by his role, not only going in first, but diving headlong into any melee. Darren Lehmann sees international cricket as involving 'pushing the boundaries', and for said boundary pushing has relied heavily on Warner, who thereby incurs constant surveillance and considerable ire. Likewise were the Australian Cricketers' Association content to have Warner last year acting as a de facto players' spokesperson in the dispute with Cricket Australia over the memorandum of understanding.

Maybe this comes naturally. But it cannot help exacting a cost. Warner's behaviour over the last few years has fluctuated markedly, something caricatured by his personae as 'The Bull' and 'The Reverend'. This is, however, no longer a joke. His combustibility around his family now smacks of a man defending his last redoubt, his only sacred ground. Those who bandy about 'the line' are ever in danger of tripping over it.

AB OR NOT AB

17 March 2018

Australia and South Africa might have been daggers drawn in Port Elizabeth last week, but one moment when hostilities abated was on the stroke of lunch on the third day when a run out ended the home side's innings.

Beginning with Mitchell Starc and including David Warner, Australians converged from all over St Georges Park to shake hands with AB de Villiers, whose undefeated 126 from 146 balls had largely built the lead that would defeat them.

While Australians have not in recent years been notable for such magnanimity, those moments when players momentarily set their game faces aside to join us in the ranks of fans are always worth cherishing. And of de Villiers, who could not be a stark, raving fan? On a pitch on which only three other fifties were scored, the South African attained a different plane.

Some shots repaid repeat viewing. There was the dead bat push from Cummins that ripped up mid-on to take him into the 30s; there were the reverse then orthodox sweeps off Lyon with which he glided through the 40s. An on-side clip off Hazelwood in the 80s was four almost before fielders turned around. A pull shot off Cummins to celebrate three figures was six on any ground in the world.

Some of the most authoritative strokes de Villiers plays, however, are defensive, for they are never entirely negative. Studies in vigilance and self-containment, they feel as dismaying to a bowler as being hit for four. Bowlers coming up against the like of Warner and Virat Kohli are often counselled to 'bowl to his ego', depriving them of the boundaries on which their self-belief feasts. De Villiers, by contrast, does not experience defence as a loss of virility or concession of weakness. He specifically dates an innings he played in Ahmedabad ten years ago — his fifth Test century and first double — for the discovery he was capable of playing such shots.

Till that point, de Villiers has explained, his approach had always been simply to hit boundaries. This day, somewhat to his surprise, he suddenly found himself playing with soft hands under his eyes. 'I feel like I can defend!' he said excitedly to his coach Mickey Arthur at a break. 'For the first time, I feel like I can defend.' Arthur apparently looked a bit non-plussed, but de Villiers was ecstatic: he had experienced dominance before, but never control.

His twenty-second Test hundred last week in Port Elizabeth, one suspects, will also come to rank high in his recollections. It was his first in more than three years, over which time he had averaged 36 in thirteen Tests, a phase elongated by a hiatus to repair body and mind after South Africa's serial failures to win a longed-for World Cup, and personal reappraisal following his wife's bearing their first child. On-going only had been de Villiers' appearances for Royal Challengers Bangalore in the Indian Premier League, worth far more than South Africa, with its struggling economy and puny rand, could possibly pay him.

De Villiers' national allegiances are assuredly strong. With Faf du Plessis, he attended Pretoria's Afrikaanse Heor Seunskool, a bastion of the Afrikaaner establishment, where boys learn by heart an Honour Code stressing 'our Language, our Nation and our Country' and the need to 'live by Christian principles'.

De Villiers made his first-class and Test debuts alongside Dale Steyn, and genuflects to Jacques Kallis, whom he says in his mind will 'always be king'. That remembered Honour Code is now supplemented by mantras: 'Watch the ball, clear mind, strong feet' for his batting, 'REPS' in his personal life (the last initial standing for 'Stay close to the Cross', reflecting his status as a believer).

Yet de Villiers has also been uncompromisingly modern in his outlook. For the last ten years, he has had not an agent, but a kind of corporate praetorian guard: wealth managers from Investec, accountants from PwC, a lawyer from Heunis & Straeuli, and a hand-picked personal assistant. The group's 'chairman' is Edward Griffiths, a former journalist and broadcast executive who became CEO of SA Rugby and more recently CEO of the Saracens.

Griffiths, sometime biographer of Kepler Wessels, Jonty Rhodes and Francois Pienaar also performed the task of ghost writer for de Villiers two years ago, in a fashion made slightly strange by a rather fundamental disagreement. Griffiths wanted to be excluded from the story. De Villiers insisted on his inclusion. Griffiths consented on condition his name was not mentioned. This led to some odd anecdotes, like one about the unidentified Griffiths taking his new charge to an empty Wanderers, asking him to imagine that it is full, and urging him to think of inspiring his countrymen by his sporting prowess: 'That is the high road, AB.'

'I realised I had reached a crossroad in my career,' wrote Griffiths in the voice of de Villiers about de Villiers reflecting on Griffiths' urgings. 'I knew I needed to take the high road.'

From detours off that high road, however, the book made clear that de Villiers had circled back to a further crossroads. 'Representing South Africa remains a massive privilege,' de Villiers averred, but with the air of someone looking back, and perhaps a little jadedly: 'If it's 100, you're a hero, if it's a 0, you are quite literally a zero. There's no point complaining; that's the reality.' India, by contrast, was 'the most inspiring place to play cricket'.

Even now de Villiers is restored as a national hero, there is a sense that it can only be temporary role — he falls into the category of another former national captain, Brendon McCullum, in the sense that his country's cricket economy is not large enough to afford him. De Villiers is thirty-four, and seemingly restored to peak proficiency. But how to optimise use to what remains? Next year's World Cup offers him a further opportunity to find something for his country's trophy cabinet — perhaps his last. Handshakes then might be of farewell.

THE RABADA AFFAIR
ANOTHER FINE MESS
23 March 2018

Historically it has been batsmen who have enjoyed the benefit of the doubt. Last week it was a bowler, Kagiso Rabada. It's far from clear he deserved it.

First of all, credit where it's due. That Dali Mpofu must be some advocate, effectively getting Rabada off something for which he'd already admitted responsibility ('It's going to have to stop because I'm letting the team down and myself'). Never mind Rumpole — that's Clarence Darrow defending Leopold and Loeb stuff.

The appeal hearing was in camera. But, dragged out over six hours, it seems to have been like one of those interminable third umpire reviews that intuition tells everyone is out but in which analysis steadily induces paralysis.

Second, bad luck Jeff Crowe, the experienced ICC referee and former Test captain, who had first found Rabada guilty of 'inappropriate and deliberate physical contact with a player' — viz Steve Smith in the Second Test. After all, it was no accident that Rabada strode down the pitch, arms aloft, exulting noisily. His eyesight, presumably, is good; his motor skills, on the evidence of his bowling, are unimpaired.

Crowe's mistake was thinking he was involved in sport, where players with prior convictions who have been warned that their actions are under scrutiny, exercise some moderation and restraint. Unfortunately for him, once South Africa appealed, and judicial commissioner Michael Heron QC parachuted in, the questions became about not cricket but law.

Heron was cajoled into regarding the contact as 'non-deliberate': assured by Rabada's counsel that no contact had been intended, the commissioner minimised the bowler's actions as 'inappropriate, lacked respect for his fellow player and involved non-deliberate and minor contact'.

But does this quite hang together? If what counts are retrospectively stated intentions, presumably Rabada did not mean the contact to be inappropriate or disrespectful either — after all, his character references are impeccable. And while volition will always be disputable, was Rabada not culpable for having 360 degrees from which to choose for the direction of his ostentatious 'celebration' and choosing the riskiest, thereby making contact likelier if not unavoidable?

Meanwhile, Heron has invented a whole new category of incident: 'minor contact'. Seriously, what the hell is that? Contact in cricket has always been, and rightly remains, taboo. 'Minor contact' makes no more sense than 'minor no-ball' and 'slightly bowled middle stump'. This judgement, then, creates an avenue for future exculpations that did not previously exist.

Just to confuse matters further, Heron gave Rabada a token ticking off for violating 'the principle that a dismissed batsman should be left alone'. Sounds like a fair principle to me. But where's it from? And why mention it if you're scarcely applying it? Maybe it's a 'minor principle'....

So Heron's is a Bob Cunis of a ruling: neither one thing nor the other, a mess of legal hair-splitting and half-remembered sporting nostrums. And presto: we have gone from zero tolerance to hero tolerance. For the loudest argument heard from South Africa in advance of the appeal was that Rabada deserved lenience because he is 'exciting', which he assuredly is, and that he is a 'role model', which would indeed be wonderful.

Yet what about those cricketers who are less exciting and perhaps not so inspiring? Do they deserve a lesser quality of justice? Surely the contrary: would not Rabada's role model status entail his being held to more exacting standards?

Most remarkable is that this was not the ICC's most egregious failure last week. The closing stages of a Nidahas Trophy T20I in Sri Lanka were degraded by protracted dissent, needless jostling, threats of forfeiture and boorishness in victory, from which ICC referee Chris Broad somehow fished two minor charges.

It was these incidents, in fact, that set the scene for South Africa's appeal, with mutterings about 'lack of consistency' in the application of the code of conduct. Actually, it was just an instance of apathetic and neglectful refereeing, but the whiney child's justification of 'but-he-got-away-with-it' needs little encouragement. Perhaps the biggest challenge in these circumstances is that the game has been perverted so regularly and the system subverted so routinely that nobody is felt to have clean hands.

Smith, I thought, coped quite impressively with the ICC's volte face, his press conference reminiscent in tone of late-model Ponting, pragmatic and sardonic, with effective application of the word 'interesting'. About send-offs, Australia's captain got in the salient point: 'What's the point of over-celebrating? And getting in the face of a batter; you've already won the battle.'

The complication for Smith is that Australia's bowlers have hardly been strangers to schadenfreude over the last five or so years. Indeed, there were widespread guffaws at the Aussie skipper, a prominent apologist for 'good, tough cricket', dispensing etiquette lessons. It wasn't long before there were chunterings of 'hypocrisy' — that parrot cry of the logically enfeebled.

Now, it *is* arguable that Smith might be better off setting his own glass house in order first. But with the view itself I can only agree. Indeed, I've always been amazed at the huffiness about Mankads, which after all punish a batsman seeking an unfair advantage, while remaining so indifferent to send-offs, which are acts of graceless gloating. Having worsened to the degree that they have come to involve physical contact, send-offs deserve to be anathematised. Perhaps, in fact, more anathema generally, and less damn 'party-of-the-first-part' code, is exactly what we need.

This last week, coincidentally, the ICC was also locked in a strategic conclave in Dubai, various committees jawboning earnestly about cricket's future. Amid the clouds of consulting jargon and the ricochet of bullet points, one imagines, the world was made a bit safer for making money. Benefit of the doubt? On the evidence of recent events, administrators deserve it least of all.

THE RABADA AFFAIR
THE STORM BEFORE THE STORM
24 March 2018

'How's your wife and my kids?' runs a classically tasteless sledge in Australian cricket folklore. Some may also be familiar with the time-honoured, politically-incorrect retort: 'The wife's fine, the kids are retarded.'

A certain innocent merriment can be derived from evaluating this exchange according to the International Cricket Council's various overlapping codes of player behaviour. It is not, arguably, 'seriously obscene'. It involves neither 'excessively audible or repetitive swearing', nor does it 'denigrate a Player ... in relation to incidents which occurred in an International Match'.

It might, all the same, conceivably 'give serious offence', and 'provoke an aggressive reaction'. Whatever the case, the Australian cricket team has in the last fortnight of a series in South Africa rendered their own somewhat counterintuitive verdict — that of it they would disapprove.

Why counterintuitive? Because for as long as anyone can remember, it has been Australians who have if not owned the copyright on sledging at least had it firmly trademarked, wearing it as an emblem of their clannishness. Their press conferences have grown almost ritualized, players defending a degree of verbal aggression on grounds it makes for 'good, tough Test cricket', while undertaking that they will not cross 'the line' — an ill-defined *cordon sanitaire*, known only to them, separating fair comment from unfair. Ten years ago it even inspired a song. 'We Never Cross the Line,' leered the white-clad chorus line of Aussie cricketers in Eddie Perfect's *Shane Warne: The Musical*. 'Calling somebody a maggot or a filthy faggot is fine.' How we laughed.

What happened during the First Test in Durban, however, may represent a watershed. Led by captain Steve Smith and vice-captain David Warner, the Australians approached their task with their usual swagger, even cheekily dropping their own sponsors' names within range of the pitch microphones to discourage the surveillances of the local broadcasters. But the Proteas are themselves no shrinking violets: what Australians call sledging, they cheerfully condone as 'chirping'.

After three and a half rankling days, some sort of confrontation seemed inevitable, with one half of it almost bound to be Warner, who relishes the role of 'keep[ing] our guys motivated on the field'. The cause

was unexpected: a sotto voce retort by South Africa's Quinton de Kock
as the teams ascended the stairs at tea referencing Warner's wife Candice
— in particular a 2007 incident in which she was photographed making
alternative use of a hotel toilet cubicle with All Black Sonny Bill Williams.

The uxorious Warner flew into a towering and sustained rage, and had
to be restrained by teammates from expressing it physically. This we know
because it was captured on CCTV footage subsequently leaked to a South
African media outlet. As it is silent, one subconsciously provides one's own
soundtrack. It is transparently not a response to 'So how's your wife and my
kids?' But whatever the provocation, it is pretty repulsive.

Hearings were heard, sentences imposed, and 'the line' made its inevitable
appearance. Copping to a fine, Warner conceded losing his temper while
defending his perspective: 'I play with aggression on the field and I try not to
cross that line … I don't think whatsoever there on the field that I have ever
crossed that line … I'll keep continuing to stick up for my family …' His hard
nut coach Darren Lehmann depicted 'the line' as a sort of chivalric code:
'When it crossed the line he defended his family and women in general, so
from my point of view I thought he did the right thing.'

But in this case, perceptions came quickly to matter more than
distinctions. One of the best responses to events in South Africa, by
Cricinfo's Sharda Ugra, not only assembled a twenty-first century Australian
rap sheet but noted the frequency with which our cricketers 'claim to be the
victims, while often being deliberate, and even skillful agent provocateurs.'

It was illustrated, inevitably, by a photograph of Warner, on Boxing Day
— chest out, striding snarlingly towards the English bowler Tom Curran,
who had had the misfortune on his Test debut to dismiss the Australian
with a no ball. 'I overheard the bowler say something,' explained Warner
afterwards. 'And I thought it was probably directed at me, it might not have
been. I found a way in there.' 'Found a way in': there's your modus operandi
right there. Warner looks for contests, seeks out vulnerabilities. A player in
his first Test who has just suffered a harrowing disappointment? The perfect
target. Smart cricket? Or the epitome of bullying?

In Durban, Smith couched support for his deputy in familiar terms:
'Quinton got quite personal and provoked an emotional response from
Davey. As far as I am aware we didn't get personal toward Quinton.' But
even softened by that politician's 'as-far-as-I-am-aware', the distinction
sounded self-serving. De Kock to Warner: 'vile slur'. Warner to Curran: 'old-
fashioned banter'. Why? Because 'the line'?

No wonder, then, that the personal/non-personal has begun to seem like a distinction without a difference. 'All sledging is personal,' observed the former Australian opener Ed Cowan in an interview on ABC radio last weekend. 'You're calling someone fat, thin, hopeless, it doesn't matter — that's a personal attack.' The line? 'I always felt that as an Australian team member, we should be nowhere near the line.'

When you're in proximity to the line, furthermore, ugly things have a way of happening. None were uglier than the two officers of Cricket South Africa who during the Second Test in Port Elizabeth took it into their heads to admit fans wearing masks of the rugby star Williams, even posing for smirking photographs with them on Twitter.

The officers were stood aside pending an 'investigation', which, frankly, need only take as long as the pair clearing their desks. But in Port Elizabeth, South Africa rather abandoned any high moral ground they had occupied in favour of a slightly shallower moral trench.

The Proteas' star bowler Kagiso Rabada incurred a two-Test suspension for, having dismissed him, brushing the shoulder of Smith as they passed: the taboo on physical contact is one that cricket *has* proved capable of preserving. After CSA lodged an appeal, a tweet appeared in the timeline of Rabada's opening partner Vernon Philander containing a counteraccusation that Smith was 'just as guilty' in the incident, and could likewise 'have avoided any contact'. Philander quickly disowned it, claiming his account had been hacked. What next? A nineteenth-century invention, Test cricket, finds itself in a twenty-first century controversy, with eavesdropping microphones and CCTV, macho posturing and slut-shaming, and social media at its most fervid and phony.

There is a tendency to say that controversy drowns cricket out. That's not entirely true. Its effects can also be magnifying and intensifying — and who would not rather watch this series, for all its abrasive edges, than another moribund Ashes? The cricket has scaled rare heights; the scenario, at one-all, could hardly be improved. Had this been a series of T20s, we'd already have played five more games and forgotten all of them.

Nor does holding the modern age up against an imagined past perfection serve much purpose. We are no likelier to return to an era of white-flannelled knights than we are the White Australia Policy. In the 1960s, when everyone was so moral and upright, our cricketers toured South Africa under apartheid — arguably a teeny bit more problematic than some cricketers swearing at each other.

No, times have changed, and actually are more challenging for a team like the Australians wrestling with a decidedly adhesive reputation. To update another old Aussie shibboleth, what happens on the field can be very hard to keep on the field when it is shared with much of the world, and all the world is positioned to offer an instant, free, partly informed and completely disinhibited opinion about it.

Because let's be straightforward here: many fans in other countries regard Australian cricketers as baggy green pricks, and, as such, fair game. That will make life no easier for them abroad; it may make it a damn sight harder. A fair proportion of fans in Australia, meanwhile, including parents in whose good graces it is important for the game to remain, aren't that rapt in them either. If your son or daughter took up a parrot cry about 'the line', how would you be disposed towards the game?

This public disgruntlement is not a recent development. Fifteen years ago, a confrontation between Glenn McGrath and the West Indian Ramnaresh Sarwan in a Test in Antigua caused such a public backlash against McGrath that the receptionist at Cricket Australia needed counselling — in those pre-social media days, people more freely picked up the phone to air their indignation. As a result, players signed up, some perhaps more willingly than others given that Lehmann was one, to a charter committing them to honour a (self-defined) 'Spirit of Cricket'. This 'Spirit', interestingly, disavowed 'sledging' but deemed 'banter between opponents and ourselves' integral to 'the competitive nature of cricket' — an antecedent, perhaps, of 'the line'.

Ten years ago, during the so-called Monkeygate affair, Ricky Ponting's Australians were surprised by their equivocal public support. When India's dignified captain Anil Kumble claimed that 'only one team was playing with the spirit of cricket', he gained a noticeable degree of public sympathy. We're now a decade's further fatigue, frustration and disaffection on, in a coarser, crueller, more combustible environment, where if you can't stand the heat then maybe you shouldn't set fire to the kitchen.

The experience may yet be salutary — a reminder that the good conduct of cricket requires rather more than superficial adherence to written codes and statutes. Both the Australians and the South Africans are coming, it is fair to say, towards the end of long seasons, which inevitably fray tempers and loosen restraints. All the same, old habits die hard, especially when they are subject to a leadership's regular reinforcement. We remain, one suspects, some distance from the Australian cricketer who will greet his opponent: 'How's your wife and your kids?'

CAPE TOWN TEST

LINES OF FIRE

26 March 2018

'The line' has been a faithful servant of Australian cricket, endlessly supple, always favourable. But its day is done. Finally, belatedly, somewhat unwillingly but at last decisively, Cricket Australia has pulled it tight.

The last time that Steve Smith and Cameron Bancroft faced the media together, in Brisbane at the end of November, it was in an atmosphere of barely-suppressed hilarity. Jonny Bairstow. The headbutt. How we laughed.

To this press conference, in Cape Town, it was actually quite difficult to listen. Bancroft was dropped in the deep end, and quickly sank. Smith deployed the standard clichés in the event of indiscretion: it was a 'poor choice'; people would 'learn something'; people would 'move on'; he would 'come back strong'. All done? Not so fast, skipper. We're not finished with you yet.

The offence is significant. If the dark arts of 'preparing' the ball for reverse swing are widely practised and any abrasive surface will do, they remain well beyond the official pale. But what's worse — more serious, more dismaying — is the combination of recklessness, sneakiness and eventual blitheness involved.

The Australians knew it was wrong. They knew it was risky. They did it anyway. They seemingly kept it from their elders. They squirmed when they were caught. They fessed up when there was no alternative. They probably believe they deserve credit for that. They don't.

The footage is desperate. Slowed down, and repeated, as it will be endlessly, probably for the next generation as representative of Australian cynicism and duplicity, it savours of vulgar calculation. It looks improvised, furtive and inept rather than cunning. But in the wider public, such distinctions are irrelevant. We cheated. We got caught. Dirt-handed. The questions didn't end with the press conference; they've barely begun.

Steve Smith is this newspaper's Australian of the Year. Did he mistake all the accolades for impunity? He has been altogether too sanguine about Australia's on-field reputation with his tiresome prattle about 'the line' and 'good, tough Test cricket.' He was evasive here in positioning himself as consulting with a 'team leadership group', whom he then all-too-cutely declined to name, that resolved the strategy. It has not saved David Warner; it may not save others. Above all, 'not proud' is not the same as ashamed, which he should be. It has been a tough tour for Smith, not making runs, not winning tricks. But character emerges in adversity, and what we have learned does not flatter him.

Nor does the involvement of Cameron Bancroft seem a fluke. He is an earnest and likeable young man desperate to play for Australia, and correspondingly desperate to endear himself to those in charge. Those in-the-know speak glowingly of his unswerving commitment to the team. His is a selection based on 'character', quietly contrasted to Matt Renshaw, who is regarded, apparently, as a little callow and self-involved.

During summer, Bancroft was observed reading a book called *The Courage to be Disliked*. From the title at least, he does not seem to have picked much up. He volunteered to cheat. His offer was accepted, with alacrity.

This speaks to team culture, and whether all the expectations of unshakeable unity and the insistence on playing to the edge of legality have not led to a dressing-room environment of corrosive conformity. Smith's 'team leadership group' — it was then David Warner, Mitchell Starc and Josh Hazelwood — were last heard of in December 2016 when they fined Glenn Maxwell for the heinous offence of nourishing ambitions to play for Australia, and admitting he was irked to be batting behind Matthew Wade for Victoria.

Maxwell, it was said, had breached the omerta. Wade, a recent Smith pick in the Australian team, had to be defended. It was all histrionic, self-dramatising nonsense. But it also exposed a cliqueiness that this Australian team is inclined to mistake for comradeship. We all know they live in a bubble — that's modern sport. But Smith's team seem just a bit too content with this state of affairs. Darren Lehmann has held the job of national coach nearly five years. He ushered the 'team leadership group' into being. He gained deserved kudos in early days for changing the culture of the Australian dressing room; but what has it changed into?

While on the subject of culture, what about corporate culture? James Sutherland's failure to read the room yesterday was almost as culpable. It was a 'very sad day'. He had 'strong and clear views' about proper behaviour. Everyone knew that. He had issued a press release about it.

Integrity? Of course CA took it seriously. They had an Integrity Unit. It would gather facts. There would be a 'process'. Had Sutherland made an attempt to ascertain the facts himself? Apparently not. Fans are at the point where they might wonder what it is Sutherland does all day. It's like he could not make a finding on the fate of the *Titanic* without a report from the Iceberg Unit.

Whoever decided to speed the process at least had a feeling for public mood, which I have never known to run as strongly against an Australian cricket team as in the last twenty-four hours. But their job is far from done. The line has outworn its usefulness, and we are in no position to be lecturing anyone any more — not, frankly, that we ever were.

CAPE TOWN TEST

FOCUS POCUS

27 March 2018

What are they thinking? What are they thinking right now? In their five-star hotel rooms, on their comfortable bus, in their fortunate, privileged, sequestered and sometimes rather lonely lives, how are Australia's cricketers feeling, about themselves, their game, their careers, their disgrace?

Contrite? Angry? Disoriented? Demoralised? Test matches render irrefutable verdicts on superiority, and defeat smarts. But one can normally fall back on the faith and love of one's home supporters. Steve Smith's team thought that their problem was with South African fans; there's nobody to complain to about their own.

Chances are that they're mainly confused. After all, from one point of view, they cut an ethical corner that is routinely side-swiped, against the team, South Africa, that is proven to have done this most often. Has every action that engendered the sometimes-extravagant degrees of reverse swing seen these series been strictly kosher? Probably not. So in that sense their misfortune was getting caught. No cameras, no problem.

Some part of them, however, will know that it is otherwise, and be aware of the odium in which they languish. They are young, impressionable, habituated to the currents of social media and the oxygen of acclaim. And this is where it will grow really confusing, in that they are being execrated for behaviours that have previously brought them rewards and approbation.

Not cheating, obviously. But their bungled ball-tampering has only been only a final step on a journey to their countrymen's disfavour. The public had already wearied of the players' unapologetic truculence, and their self-justifying protestations that they just play cricket the Aussie way.

A common chain of reasoning since the Australians' admission has been to wonder why senior and junior team members slipped so heedlessly into malpractice. Did they not pause? Did they not reflect? Did they not consider that what they were doing was technically illegal, morally wrong, potentially disastrous?

No: and not, I think, because they are particularly wicked or conscienceless, but because that capacity to find an advantage, to simplify and compartmentalize, to live entirely in the moment, forgetting the past and ignoring posterity, is routinely called 'focus', and exalted to the skies.

Focus is, by definition, an act of narrowing, and narrowing is the essence of modern professional sport, which excels at nurturing specimens who will subordinate all to the business of skill acquisition and constant surveillance, the pursuit of individual excellence and collective goals. Ethics is readily compromised, deemed superfluous. And victory, of course, excuses everything.

It has become quite a jarring experience to listen to Australian cricketers over the last few years. They have come to sound almost absurdly alike. Part of this is an outcome of the stultifyingly boring lives they lead and the sterilisation of their interaction with the outside world, consisting chiefly of media conferences where they pretend to talk and we pretend to listen. But at times the team has sounded almost cult-like, repeating a monotonous chant about 'good, hard Test cricket', 'opening scars/cracks', and our old friend 'the line', the 'head-butting' thereof.

David Warner has always exhibited a tendency to such free associations, but others have slipped into similar vein. On the eve of the First Ashes Test, for example, Nathan Lyon, once a refreshingly affable contrast to the norm, went off on a frankly weird jag about his 'scared' English opponents: 'Could we end some careers? I hope so.' It was like listening to a ventriloquist's dummy.

Is this, one has wondered, how cricketers get on? Is it why a Matthew Wade supplants a Peter Nevill? Is it why players with minds of their own, a Glenn Maxwell or a George Bailey, do not seem to progress? Is this why a Cameron Bancroft receives such praise for his unswerving dedication to 'the team'? Has selection become a search not for talent but for type? After all, the coach is a selector, and where 'the line' is concerned he is the greatest proselytizer of all.

I had the opportunity to interview Bancroft eighteen months ago, at some length. Nice lad. Courteous. Thoughtful. Had played trumpet at high school. Cherished the opportunity to play The Last Post because of an uncle who had served in Vietnam. Interesting things to say. Said them well.

Also desperately perfectionistic; to an almost disconcerting degree consumed by his career. The kind of young man who if asked by a coach would run through a brick wall; not the kind who would reply: 'If the idea is to get the other side, coach, why don't I just walk around it?' As we parted, I felt strangely worried for him. How would he cope if he did not achieve what he wanted? How would he cope if he did?

So by all means pillory these cricketers. They deserve it. They have been foolish, wilful, sneaky, and hypocritical. But don't omit the role of the system that fostered them, that demands 'high-performance' rather than high ethical standards, that is concerned for their welfare only for so long as they remain of use, and will discard them unsentimentally when they are done.

Because the other group that did not see this coming is Cricket Australia, despite their own weird cult of 'fans first', which is actually shorthand for 'consumers first', and in which the game of cricket often seems a concern anterior to the monetising of same. What are they thinking? Because they have a very great deal to think about.

BALL TAMPERING

MEET THE SUITS

31 March 2018

After the Hobart Test of November 2016 ended with Australia bowled out twice in little more than 90 overs, the atmosphere in the home dressing room was suitably funereal.

Australia had sustained five consecutive Test defeats at home and abroad. Five team members were about to lose their places. Chairman of selectors Rod Marsh had already handed in his commission; captain Steve Smith walked in from a post-match press conference where he'd admitted feeling 'embarrassed to be sitting here.'

On this private grief, two others were about to intrude. Cricket Australia CEO James Sutherland and general manager team performance Pat Howard held the floor, incongruous in their dark jackets and ties amid the cricketers and support staff in their official gear. And they were scathing: losing like this was not an option.

Smith, as he describes in his autobiography, had never seen Sutherland and Howard together in such a context: 'It's not something I'd experienced before in my career and I hope it's not something I'll ever experience again.' It was less what the executives said than the height that they said it from. 'If you get a dressing-down from what you would describe as "suits",' noted Smith, 'then you know things have gone badly off the rails.'

Last week in South Africa, the suits were back, and the rails led over a cliff. Sutherland arrived with Howard to pronounced sentence on Smith, his deputy David Warner, and Warner's opening partner Cameron Bancroft, who will ever be stained as cheats and liars. No sooner had they departed than coach Darren Lehmann was foreshadowing his last Test in charge, it being 'the right time to step away' — that is, before he was pushed. The Australian team's crisis of form in 2016, bad as it seemed at the time, was as nothing compared to its current crisis of reputation.

But are the two related? Have the intolerance of failure, the exaltation of success, the arrogance of wealth and an *idée fixe* with commercial outcomes led to this dead end of execration and exile? After all, there was a certain irony in Sutherland's rediscovery of the 'spirit of cricket' which last year was quietly dropped from CA's published strategy, replaced by a compound of jaded slogans about 'how we play': 'Be real, smash the boundaries, make every ball count, stronger together.'

At times over the years, CA has given the appearance of caring little about the sport's image, except as a brand or a product. One was reminded last week of the conference five years ago where CA's commercial chief Ben Amarfio argued that controversy in sport was not a problem — it could even be advantageous. Citing rights deals signed by the Australian Football League and National Rugby League amid cycles of negative publicity about drugs, violence and corruption, Amarfio argued that 'noise' in 'the media' actually created 'a lot more interest in your brand and your sport' by generating 'a lot of discussion and debate'. Now that he is pitching Australian cricket to suddenly sceptical broadcasters, Channel Nine having opted for nice wholesome Australian Open, and that a hard-won Test sponsor has quit, Magellan having terminated its relationship two years early, one wonders how Amarfio's thesis is shaping up.

Lehmann was cleared of direct involvement in the short cuts the players took in attempting to doctor the ball during the Third Test. Yet before the Test series, Lehmann appeared quite sanguine about such practices: 'Obviously there's techniques used by both sides to get the ball reversing. That's just the way the game goes. I have no problem with it. Simple.' For the last few years, Warner has been in charge of Australia's handling and management of the ball, and is now held chiefly responsible for Bancroft's crude and inept attempts to do the same. But given his coach's public attitudes, he might conceivably have felt he had carte blanche.

Nobody, meanwhile, was identified more closely than Lehmann with the roughhouse style of cricket from which CA is now backpedalling like a terrified tailender facing a fast bowler. In the end it hardly mattered whether or not his fingerprints were on the sandpaper.

Let's a take a step back, as all these figures are interlinked. Sutherland, a tall, grave and rather shy figure who wears a jacket and tie like a suit of armour, has been CEO for nearly seventeen years, during which the organisation's revenues have grown more than ten-fold. Howard, with a background in property and rugby, and Amarfio, from radio and football, were recruited in 2011 and 2012 respectively, as part of an executive makeover.

At the time, the Australian team was rebuilding, falteringly, as the last remnants of a great generation moved on. CA were launching new attractions, notably a bold domestic T20 competition, the Big Bash League, and in the market for new stars.

Warner, newly launched on his way through T20, made a perfect fit. In some respects, brash, volatile and suggestible, he is a more completely modern figure than even Smith. Warner also presented management challenges. Indeed, it was his loss of control one infamous night at the Walkabout in Birmingham in June 2013 that made for Lehmann's ascension as coach.

Installing Lehmann in place of the hapless Mickey Arthur, Sutherland could hardly have been clearer about where the buck stopped: 'Discipline, consistency of behaviour and accountability for performance are all key ingredients that need to improve. And we see that the head coach is ultimately responsible for that.' Yet one of the sharpest appraisals of Australia's predicament came last week from Arthur, now coach of Pakistan, who in a post on the website *Players' Voice* argued that the deterioration in the Australian team and organisational culture was 'always going to end like this.'

'I have been bitterly disappointed watching the Australian cricket team over the last few years,' Arthur wrote. 'The behaviour has been boorish and arrogant. The way they've gone about their business hasn't been good, and it hasn't been good for a while. I know what my Pakistani players were confronted with in Australia two summers ago. I heard some of the things said to the English players during the Ashes. It was scandalous.'

Sooner or later, Arthur argued, the culture was bound to eat its own: 'Despite generational change, independent reviews and too many behavioural spot fires to list, Cricket Australia and the national team had demonstrated no real willingness or desire to improve the culture within their organisation from season to season. That could lead to only one conclusion. An explosion.'

An explosion it has been, and it's important to recognise that while Smith, Warner and Bancroft have been punished for specific offences under CA's code of conduct, the sentences have been calibrated according to public indignation, which itself is inflamed by a sense of accumulated misdeeds and annoyances.

It is a strength of cricket that Australians feel such an intense sense of connection with and proprietorship of the national team. It is why they experienced such a personal sense of loss three and half years ago on the death of Phillip Hughes. That also makes it a fraught relationship. Australians have high expectations of their cricketers. They want to look up to and feel proud of them. They want to see them embodying special values, national traits.

Some thought that Hughes' tragic death might prelude a kinder, gentler game. New Zealand's cricketers, who were playing a Test against Pakistan at the time, were deeply affected, as their captain Brendon McCullum recalled in his autobiography: 'It was so strange, yet felt so right, that after Phil's death, we didn't really care about the result. The fact that nothing we could or couldn't do on the field really mattered … had an amazingly liberating effect.'

Australian cricket experienced harrowing grief, but no liberation. Perhaps it would have involved too much soul-searching: sport here defaults readily to ersatz machismo. When they were opposed in the World Cup three years ago, in fact, Australians roundly mocked the Black Caps' approach. Keeper Brad Haddin insisted that McCullum's New Zealanders 'deserved' to be sledged as viciously as possible because they were 'nice', which he regarded as a deliberate ploy to make the Australians 'uncomfortable'.

(Irony alert: one of Lehmann's thought bubbles last week involving taking 'a leaf out of someone like, say, New Zealand's book, the way they play and respect the opposition', the inference being that this for Australians would be a new experience. Haddin, meanwhile, is Australia's fielding coach).

So the team marched on, precluded from real introspection by dumb obedience and relentless scheduling: since the World Cup 38 Tests, 56 one-day internationals, 23 T20 internationals, with Smith and Warner involved for all but a handful. All with, it must be said, the full consent of their bosses. 'In my view I don't think we have too many troubles at all,' said Howard in October 2016 when Michael Clarke spoke of a cultural malaise in the Australian team set-up. 'I am very happy with how the guys get on together, it's very strong and I haven't got any concerns in that space.'

Howard is an energetic and meticulous technocrat, with a propensity for spitting out data reminiscent of Mr Memory in *The Thirty-Nine Steps*. He is also oblivious to his limitations and dismissive of criticism, perhaps overcompensating for his lack of cricket background. He formed a tight unit with Lehmann and also with national talent manager Greg Chappell, who returned to the selection panel after Rod Marsh's resignation. And they enjoyed just enough success to keep doubt at bay.

Nor were Smith and Warner, captain and vice-captain, the types to lead cultural change.

Smith's boyish exterior hides … well, a boyish interior. He lives for cricket, which is just as well because the system offers him nothing else, except money, in quantities barely meaningful anyway. He owns shares in racehorses he has never watched live; he follows the Roosters but never gets to games. Smith is a virtuoso batting soloist. Interpersonal relations occur at a pitch he does not quite hear. While his predecessor Clarke coveted control of his team in all its aspects, Smith has relied heavily on Lehmann, and an increasingly crowded back room. In the ascendant, Smith has looked unassailable. Under pressure, he has sometimes appeared brittle. From Sri Lanka in 2016, where he grew increasingly besieged and brooding, he was sent home early. In India last year, he suffered a notorious 'brain fade' with the decision review system at Bengaluru, and vehemently denounced an opponent for claiming a catch on the bounce at Dharamsala.

Warner is, meanwhile, as Warner does, and has had a consistent enabler in Lehmann. On the field, Australia's vice-captain has provided their abrasive competitive surface; off it, his coach has smoothed things over. When Warner was fined after a confrontation with India's Rohit Sharma in a one-day international, for example, Lehmann dismissed it as 'just the tail end of some chat that had been going on for a while'.

Warner embraced his role as Lehmann's agent provocateur variously — at times with a manic glee, at other times with seeming reservations. A year ago in India, for example, Warner seemed almost withdrawn, and his batting form attenuated accordingly.

What then broke the nexus of players and overseers was last year's pay dispute between CA and the Australian Cricketers' Association as the representative of the country's elite male and female cricketers. The dispute was not so much about the top players as it was about rank-in-file domestic cricketers and their entitlement to partake directly of a proportion of revenue. But the campaign, which roiled for nine months, was costly and divisive. The ubiquitous Howard was instrumental in CA's negotiations until Sutherland's belated involvement. Smith publicly endorsed the ACA's position, while Warner was drawn regularly and sometimes unwisely into the fray.

The dispute's resolution in the ACA's favour was a humiliation for CA and perhaps also a reinforcement for the players. Certainly, as summer began, Warner seemed to carry himself with renewed swagger, returning to his accustomed role against a favoured opponent — in Australian eyes, all is fair against England. Quarry perceived to be vulnerable and inexperienced, such as Jonny Bairstow and Tom Curran, were singled out for particular attention.

In this, again, Warner had full institutional backing. The Ashes were replete with malicious glee, whether it was CA's overeager media arm tizzying up nonsensical ball-tampering stories against James Anderson in Melbourne or CA's dunderhead marketers and their crass mobile presentation stage in Sydney. No thought of the 'spirit of cricket' then; just

Ben Amarfio's lip-smacking relish for 'controversy'.

Especially given the Australians' pre-series insistence on the fading of stump mics, one suspects that Warner was similarly primed in South Africa. His visible targets were quietly-spoken Quinton de Kock and new cap Aiden Markram. But South Africa, team and country, presented a harder target. Opponents were more skilful, crowds more confronting. Smith and Warner were neutralised on the field and antagonised off it. Both developed man-eating grievances: Smith about the escape from suspension of his nemesis Kagiso Rabada, Warner about the disgusting vilification of his wife Candice. They were playing like angry men, yet nobody in that amply-resourced and hugely experienced coaching staff seems to have intuited this and been capable of taking action. On the contrary, Lehmann sided decisively with Warner when the Australian vice-captain had his confrontation with de Kock: 'When it crossed the line he defended his family and women in general, so from my point of view I thought he did the right thing.'

Smith and Warner made, we know now, disastrous personal choices, in doing so implicating an inexperienced teammate. This has been the story's most damaging dimension, that Bancroft fell in so holus-bolus with the conspiracy. Yet Bancroft was in his way the system's most studious disciple — cricket's equivalent of the company man, carefully nurtured and promoted, encouraged and lauded for his self-sacrificing dedication to the team culture.

So the 'suits' arrived to pass judgement on the system they helped build and the individuals they effectively groomed, ridding themselves into the bargain of the troublesome Warner. Trailed now is 'an independent review into the conduct and culture of our Australian men's teams'. At the moment it is no more than a wish, and the precedents are unpromising. When CA held an allegedly independent review of its men's teams seven years ago, interviewees were astonished to find Sutherland sitting in on their interviews.

It is far from clear, moreover, that the review should stop with the teams. Indeed, it is telling how rapidly CA has found itself deserted by stakeholders and partners in this affair — not one has been heard in support. For many years CA have looked on enviously at their crosstown rival the Australian Football League; they now find themselves equally unloved, but with an inferior story to tell and sell. Who will judge the suits for that? Because someone must.

THE LOVE OF CRICKET
WHY IT STILL MATTERS
31 March 2018

A week ago, I was in Nyora in Gippsland, a town of fewer than 1000 people that puts into the field two senior and a junior cricket teams on a picturesque oval.

Nyora CC has battled back from a brink a few years back, led by a coach who is an old mate of mine. I was a guest at their presentation night, and had, as I seldom fail to at such gatherings, a great time, with solid cricket people. There was, as they say, a lot of love in that room.

Afterwards, the coach and I adjourned to his couch for some cricket watching … and suddenly turned to each other, eyes on stalks.

What. Just. Happened?

Actually what had happened was pretty obvious, which paradoxically was what made it difficult to take in. Ball tampering has usually been evidenced by blurry photographs of furtive fingers worrying at balls and seams, not crystal clear live footage amenable to super slo-mo.

In the statute book, at least, tampering has remained a relative trifle, certainly compared to fixing and doping. But here the offence was magnified by its being so vivid, so avid, so downright clumsy.

My phone began to ping, and has not stopped, in a week of outrage unexampled in my sports writing experience, to which my colleagues and I have contributed our share, but rather a lot of which emerged organically.

Certainly I have never received such a volume of correspondence where opinion has run so strongly one way. There is a degree of self-selection to this: those motivated to write will be drawn disproportionately from the disaffected. But I was struck by the uniformly pained and long-suffering tone of these communications: this was, for many, in the nature of a 'last straw', after a protracted estrangement from a team they'd lost faith in.

At the same time, people don't write or sound off about what they don't care about, and in this respect they had perhaps more in common with the objects of their ire than they knew. The players and the coach in their mea culpas all used the word 'love' when they talked about their relationship to cricket. I don't think that's a coincidence; nor is it invention or hyperbole.

I'm aware of the passion engendered by other games, but I'm prepared here to make a claim for the uniqueness of the love of cricket. One simply does not love tennis or golf or even football the same way, even though they all matter equally — a lot and hardly at all.

There's the love of cricket's complexity, the fascination exerted by the intricacy, variety and subtlety of its skills.

There's the love of its romance, of the elaborateness of its rituals, of its ineffability and mysteriousness to outsiders, of its heritage and continuity in the national story.

There's the love of its difficulty — the perverse affection that arises from it being so challenging and frustrating, for offering even the poorest practitioner a glimpse of the possible, for leaving at times even the greatest so helpless.

There is also the love of its spirit. Sometimes this is travestied as an appeal for gentility — effete, pommy nonsense, all garden parties and cucumber sandwiches.

This is a misunderstanding. The spirit expresses a grasp of the need, as cricket is constituted and regulated, for restraint and reciprocity. As the Indian sociologist Ashis Nandy has noted, cricket is 'almost unique in providing ample scope for unjust play as well as having strong taboos against such play.' Participants are quietly but bindingly committed to doing the right thing, by each other and by the game.

It takes only one player to disrupt and ruin a cricket match. Two or three, as we have seen, and the game has no chance. In that sense cricket will always be in danger of plunging into chaos; it is a source of constant wonder to me that it does not do so more often.

This is actually a very different 'love' to the kind that Cricket Australia has been selling these last few years, which has been an attempt, through the Big Bash League, to introduce to cricket a version of the tribalism of football. It is accessible; it is fun; it is lucrative; but it relates to love about as deeply as *The Bachelor in Paradise* does.

It is also a very different kind of love to that expressed toward the game this week by cynical and exploitative politicians — Malcolm Turnbull cocking his tin popular ear to this story may have been just about its low point — and the craven, self-serving sponsors who quickly made for the hills.

Commonwealth Bank cutting Steve Smith — now there's a laugh, because frankly it could just as easily, and more properly, have been the other way round. For all that he has erred, Smith can tell right from wrong; Commonwealth Bank has spent years wringing profits from serial violations of the law and common decency. Perhaps this is not the time to pick and choose, but cricket has gone too long helping the Commonwealth Bank launder its filthy reputation.

While I listened sympathetically to the plaints of others, I outraged out pretty quickly on this story. Professionally, I was obliged to feed the beast of opinion; personally, I'd just as soon have turned away, from the spiralling indignation, and the squalid business of public shaming. To watch Steve Smith in tears and Cameron Bancroft in anguish felt voyeuristic, predatory.

The desire to isolate, concentrate and punish the guilty was in part about the absolution of others who turned a blind eye to a worsening culture and reputation. It's not David Warner's fault alone that we have a team so widely disliked; there have been others perfectly comfortable with this because they thought it worked in our favour. It's not Cam Bancroft's fault alone that he did what was asked; it's what the culture encouraged him to do, even celebrated him for.

But it's self-indulgent in these circumstances to give way to anger and dismay, not if you truly love the game. Sadly, perhaps, cricket's not always going to make you happy. Sometimes it will disappoint, dismay and depress you: it's as straight only as the crooked bat willow of humanity. But love finds a way to rise above that, and there's lots of it out there. I can recommend a visit to Nyora, Steve. You'd get a real kick out of it.

AUSTRALIA IN SOUTH AFRICA

CULTURE VULTURES

7 April 2018

Harpo speaks!

It was a Friday afternoon, in Brisbane, down the road from a Commonwealth Games, ahead of a big sporting weekend. But the novelty of hearing from Cricket Australia's sunken-profile chairman David Peever was almost as enticing as anything he actually said.

The nub, delivered in a studious monotone, was a confirmation that CA, having first flagged 'an independent review into the conduct and culture of our Australian men's team' following events in South Africa, would be conducting 'a review of the wider context of the event' in case 'wider cultural, organisational and/or governance issues need to be addressed'.

Why? Because he had to. That's not my opinion. It was the opinion of the last review of the Australian team, in 2011, chaired by businessman Don Argus.

The very fact of the appointment of Argus, with a record of zero Test runs at an average of 0.0, made concrete the case that the Australian team and its management were inextricably linked.

Argus followed that predetermination through to its logical conclusion by making his centrepiece recommendation the creation of a new management position, general manager team performance — a role held since by Pat Howard.

The responsibilities for this general manager could hardly have been more explicit: 'Execution of agreed plans in coaching, team leadership, culture and selection.' Any review of 'culture' had, therefore, to include Howard.

The Argus review's assertion that Howard's position was 'ultimately accountable' for the team, furthermore, was elaborated by a footnote to the effect that 'of course the CEO and ultimately, the Board, remain accountable too'. Just fancy that.

This ultimate ultimately was depicted in a helpful management diagram on page 12 — tilted on its side to accommodate all the important-sounding titles — with short thick lines connecting boxes that read 'GM Team Performance', 'CA CEO' and 'CA board'. QED.

That the crisis in South Africa sprang as much from the reputation of our cricketers as from their specific misdemeanours further deepened the need for a comprehensive review.

Rather like the national team it has put in the field in recent years, CA is perceived in sporting, commercial and media circles, and increasingly by the public, as arrogant, as confrontational, as intolerant of criticism, and as living in a bubble.

This profile, by the way, is not wholly fair, and certainly disserves many excellent, motivated and conscientious staff members. But what were CA's involvement in the big-three heist at the International Cricket Council and CA's support for a 10-team World Cup but the ugliest kind of political bullying?

David Warner sledging Quinton de Kock on the field and David Peever sledging a CBS executive by email, as reported on Thursday, aren't separated by that great a gulf.

Perhaps the chief difference is that Warner now languishes under a year's suspension, while Peever continues his plush sinecure despite chairing Cricket Australia through two of the most damaging controversies in Australian cricket's history. What else might be learned from the last review that might be germane to the next?

The curious thing is that people periodically revert to Argus as though on the basis of a few months' work seven years ago he remains some sort of expert on the subject.

This newspaper did a week ago, when it reported him as blaming player misbehaviour on an 'assumption of entitlement', cricketers believing their 'wealth' to be 'a right not a reward'. Savour the irony of a corporate chieftain who backed his truck up for decades opining on entitlement culture.

Actually, it would be worth someone pulling the 'Australian Team Performance Review' out from under whichever desk it is holding steady for some guidance about what the next report should avoid.

Most importantly, CA is now promising an 'independent review'. Alas, if the 'independent' Argus Review is any guide, they need a better dictionary.

Argus's colleagues were Malcolm Speed (former CA CEO), Mark Taylor (CA director), Allan Border (former CA director) and Steve Waugh (previous Australian captain but one). Able individuals all, it could be claimed, but also tied by history and sentiment to the status quo.

Sutherland, moreover, was as an 'ex-officio, non-voting member' of the review group, entitling him to attend meetings, ask questions and influence outcomes, while the secretariat was composed of CA staff. In other words, the exercise could be regarded as marginally more 'independent' than East Germany under Erich Honecker.

To be genuinely meaningful and authoritative, the next review needs to be credibly arms-length, and seen to be so, led by someone who knows the ropes but isn't tied to them.

There are also few areas the review CA needs should not go into. A useful step would be soliciting feedback on the external experience of its organisational culture from all stakeholders, including the state associations, sponsors, suppliers, media, and peer boards overseas.

The review should evaluate the culture of selection, its integrity slowly corroded by the involvement of the coach and the national talent manager, essentially in the position of grading their own work, and a selector who somehow also acts as a television commentator but otherwise displays desultory interest in watching cricket. The review might usefully contemplate the values implied when, for example, national selectors call up cricketers under suspension by their states.

The review should scrutinise the culture of a pathways system obsessed with speed, power, revs and X-factor to the exclusion of actual performance, perhaps because shaping raw talent is a way for coaches, sports scientists and other data-driven dittoheads to advance, and because consistency and character are sooooo 20th century.

The review should examine ... well, basically it should examine what it wants, with open terms of reference that aren't engineered to reach preordained outcomes — something of which the Argus review contained more than a glint.

The decision last week by Warner, Steve Smith and Cameron Bancroft not to challenge their sentences made CA's job easier and harder. They've accepted accountability for their actions. Now it's the turn of administrators, whose philosophies have in recent times been reminiscent of that line of Harpo's brother. 'Those are my principles,' stated Groucho famously. 'And if you don't like them ... well, I have others.'

A NEW COACH

JUSTIN TIME

5 May 2018

Meet the new boss. Same as the old boss?

Justin Langer and Darren Lehmann were born in the same year, formed part of the same era of cricket dominance, bristled with the same Australian aggression, have coached many of the same players in similar settings.

Normally such continuity would offer the reassuring guarantee of a seamless transition; but given that there seems at least a public mandate for change, that may not be altogether a blessing.

On the other hand, when Langer acted as Lehmann's locum last summer, he was apparently underwhelmed by the dressing room atmosphere — the lack of enthusiasm, the sense of coasting. If any coach is likely to shake a group out of that, it is strength-through-joy Justin, disciple of flinty Steve Waugh, adherent of Dennis Lillee's three-part creed for cricket success: hard work, hard work and hard work.

There was something for everyone in Langer's debut press conference as Australian coach this week. Not all of it, therefore, was entirely coherent.

Langer offered us an Australian cricket clannish about 'elite mateship', yet also welcoming of those 'a bit different'. He favoured a culture all about winning yet also all about creating good people. There are always balances to be struck, yet it was not altogether obvious where these were.

Australians, Langer explained, have always played 'good, hard, competitive cricket', while also knowing 'what the acceptable behaviours are'. Except that recent evidence suggests the contrary, and some would say that this has applied for quite a while.

Steve Smith and Cameron Bancroft, Langer insisted, 'love the game more than anyone I know and they are great kids'. Except that their actions in South Africa showed not love for cricket but contempt, and they are not 'kids', being adults, aged 28 and 25 respectively.

Let's be fair. A new coach outlining his vision is a little like an idealistic politician on the hustings. It is about including everyone, tackling everything, blending big and small, past and future. Langer has an appealing, invigorating feel for the country's cricket heritage. His knowledge is immense and his passion contagious.

Langer comes with rare credentials as a motivator. He has a winning way in person and in print, toiling hard over the writing of three books, and gleaning lessons from many more.

There's also been a lot to admire in the way Langer plunged into coaching — headlong, the hard way, exactly as he played, without compromise, and sometimes with a touch of anger.

All the same, his success in the west has been of a particular kind. He was here an established legend, casting a long shadow and cracking a thick whip over a talented but indolent squad.

In his time, the Scorchers have become Australia's T20 benchmark, perhaps the world's. Nonetheless, despite comparatively few international calls, Western Australia's Sheffield Shield drought has stretched to twenty years: last season they finished fourth, winning only one away game. He has not, then, achieved every ambition at which he's aimed — although he may be better for it.

A note of caution may be in order. Amid last week's optimism were also detectable hints of a besetting sin in Australian cricket, which is arrogance — the arrogance that irks broadcasters, sponsors, suppliers and bilateral partners alike; the arrogance that has Cricket Australia's chairman no sooner launching a cultural review than pre-empting its findings by saying that he's 'not going anywhere' and that his CEO's job is 'safe'.

'One of the things we've got in Australian cricket unlike other countries is that we've got great players,' Langer insisted at one point. 'Not just really good players, or good players. But we've got great players and we're lucky to draw on those … Not many countries have that luxury.'

Errrr, coach, other countries have great players too. Most of them actually. And having past masters around can't mean that much, otherwise the West Indies, with probably more former greats per capita than any international team, would still rule the roost.

This was an odd assertion, too, because the coach himself did not learn at the feet of a luminary. Langer's career-long mentor has been Scarborough's unassumingly excellent Noddy Holder; his consistent and commendable attitude has been treating every encounter as holding the potential for learning. Let's hope he reverts to it, rather than narrowing his gaze to mere ancestor worship.

In response to a question, Cricket Australia's CEO James Sutherland then revealed that the search for Lehmann's successor had gone no further than the ranks of countrymen. Why? Because 'the top half dozen coaches in the world are Australian'.

Hmm, big call from the third-ranked Test team and fifth-ranked one-day international team who, despite all our manifold advantages and resources, haven't won a series in England since 2001, or in Asia since 2011.

Is it even true? After all, South Africans Gary Kirsten and Mickey Arthur have each taken two international teams to the top of the Test rankings. New Zealand's Mike Hesson does an excellent job with scant resources, while his compatriots Stephen Fleming and Daniel Vettori have coached successfully all over the world. Ditto the West Indians Ottis Gibson and Phil Simmons.

Which is not to say that any of the foregoing would have been better choices than Langer — simply that in the decade since the end of our long run atop the Test ladder, we have retrieved that status for a total of nine months (May-July 2014, February to August 2016).

We talk up our aim of being number one in all three formats, but we're not within several postcodes of it, and until next April will be without our two best batsmen. Wonder how our rankings will look this time next year ....

An observable reality of the last month has been the outsized pleasure many have taken in Australia's calamities — the sense that we've had it coming, that we dish it out but can't take it, that we prefer talk to listening and data to wisdom. Back in the day we consoled ourselves that we were disliked for being good; now we're less good, we might have to face up to not being very likeable.

That's a shame. With one sentiment last week, Justin Langer struck a strong chord. He talked about the importance of Australian cricketers 'earning respect'. For too long we have demanded it as a matter of course; a fruitful first step to its rebuilding will be humility. The public won't get fooled again.

JAMES SUTHERLAND DEPARTS

THE 17-YEAR ITCH

6 June 2018

Cricket Australia chairman David Peever began his encomia for his departing CEO James Sutherland with an impressive set of empirical measures of cricket's growth in his seventeen-year tenure. One-hundred-and-thirty-seven per cent this. Ten-fold that. A 228 per cent increase in participation.

Not 227, or 229, mark you: 228. The calculation of such figures is always somewhat mysterious, but they gain an authority from their precision and repetition. Sutherland is an accountant by training — not that there's anything wrong with that. But sometimes in his tenure, cricket seemed more obsessed with quantity than quality.

The foreshadowing of his departure, likewise, is narrowly rationalised. Yes, the preparation of a new strategic plan, the conclusion of a collective bargain and the signing of a broadcasting deal were important.

But CA has just begun what it is presenting as a root-and-branch of its organisational culture after the gravest behavioural infractions of Sutherland's career. Captain, vice-captain, coach, selector, director, integrity manager: Australian cricket has been turning personnel over like a circus car disgorging clowns.

In these circumstances, stable and unambiguous leadership would surely have been advantageous; instead, CA is led by effectively a lame duck, with a year's speculation to come.

The notice period, in fact, reflects poorly on a board that has effectively had six years to groom a successor and failed to do so, and a chairman who has spent two years aware of the finitude of Sutherland's time and seemingly done damn all.

Let's give Sutherland credit. He is a decent, likeable man, hard-working and well-motivated. That he presented in public as woodenly as David Warner's Kaboom was strangely endearing. Sutherland wasn't slick, or glib, or even particularly polished, and never dealt happily with the media, which in some ways is preferable to phony bonhomie.

Formality became him. Seeing Sutherland at a T20 international ten years ago without a tie was like catching Paul Keating in thongs. It was helpful too. Appointed in 2001 at the age of only thirty-five, Sutherland inherited a tricky, factionated, federal governance system full of grizzled, leathery and considerably older men, and dealt with it patiently and diplomatically. If he did not always hold the solution to problems, he had a gift for identifying, quarantining and trading them off.

Sutherland benefited from historic endowments. The emergence of a uniquely talented generation of young players in the late 1980s and early 1990s, mainly incubated at Adelaide's Cricket Academy, preluded a period of unexampled on-field strength. To his successor, Sutherland will bequeath financial strength, embodied in the men's and women's Big Bash Leagues, which are weaning CA off its troublesome dependence on distributions from ICC events, and the Ashes and Border-Gavaskar Trophy cycles. It is a considerable legacy.

Integral to understanding him is that Sutherland came to office so early in his life, as a recent player and a new father. The cricket aspirations of son Will and daughter Annabel gave him a special perspective on the challenges of enthusing the young, not least the game's limited availability to women — the view he expressed yesterday that 'the most important thing we do as sports administrators is inspire the next generation to love cricket' was heartfelt and sincere.

At the same time, Sutherland had necessarily limited executive experience, and little opportunity thereafter to develop it. He referred yesterday to the 'talent and passion of my work colleagues'. Yet, to few did he seem personally close: he was not a floor walker or an open-door manager. It was a standing joke that Sutherland would have preferred to run CA by email, seeing nobody.

It is notable that in seventeen years there has never been real pressure from below Sutherland — a stand-out figure who presented as a future CEO. Executives came and went or stayed and stagnated. Sutherland can also be faulted for failing to attend to Jolimont's deteriorating working conditions and ceaseless turf wars. CA's senior executive is arguably overpaid and its junior staff frankly underpaid, while its reputation with external stakeholders has worsened from average to poor.

Cricket's public has expanded significantly, as the game has been rendered more accessible, which can only be good. As a result, however, the audience is more fragmented, readily confused and potentially volatile.

For years, CA has preened itself about putting 'fans first'. Yet it seemed indifferent or impervious to discontent about the national team which during the ball tampering affair finally vented. Cricket has gained its new following at some expense to its abiding hold on Australian imagination.

Last year CA fought a divisive and destructive industrial relations battle with its players, at a heavy cost to their profile as well as its, ostensibly driven by the urgent needs of grassroots cricket. Nine months on, there is little evidence of a strategy to meet said needs.

In his time, then, Sutherland has helped make cricket a more prosperous sport, more robust and diverse in its revenues, shinier and noisier in its forms. But as even accountants are sometimes told, not everything that matters can be measured, and not everything that can be measured matters.